"*Releasing Our Burdens* is a profound offering in these times of cumulative overwhelm. Dick Schwartz and Thomas Hübl gently guide us into the space where individual, ancestral, and collective healing meet—where presence becomes a path to compassionate unburdening. This book honors the intelligence of our trauma responses while inviting us to metabolize legacy pain through connection and deep inner resonance. A timely, soulful integration of relational neuroscience, somatic work, and ancestral wisdom."

Linda Thai
trauma therapist and educator

"Brilliant and immediately helpful. These days we hear a lot about trauma. This compelling book actually shows how it can be healed. Practical, compassionate, and wise."

Dr Jack Kornfield
author of *A Path with Heart* and *All in This Together*

Also By Dr Richard C. Schwartz

No Bad Parts: Healing Trauma and Restoring Wholeness with the Internal Family Systems Model

Introduction to Internal Family Systems

You Are the One You've Been Waiting For: Applying Internal Family Systems to Intimate Relationships

Internal Family Systems Therapy, 2nd edition (with Martha Sweezy)

Family Therapy: Concepts and Methods, 7th edition (with Michael P. Nichols)

The Mosaic Mind: Empowering the Tormented Selves of Child Abuse Survivors (with Regina A. Goulding)

Metaframeworks: Transcending the Models of Family Therapy (with Douglas C. Breunlin and Betty Mac Kune-Karrer)

Handbook of Family Therapy Training and Supervision (with Howard A. Liddle and Douglas C. Breunlin)

Praise for *Releasing Our Burdens*

"*Releasing Our Burdens* is a lantern that illuminates the complex path of healing layered trauma. This book is a living companion, offering an intentional interweaving of individual, ancestral, and collective healing. With compassion and depth, it gently guides readers through the heavy terrains of emotional pain, reminding us that both personal and collective integration are indeed possible."

Dr Mariel Buqué
bestselling author of *Break the Cycle*, creator of BTC Generational Trauma Therapy™

"*Releasing Our Burdens* is a deeply integrative work that resonates with the truth that trauma does not live only in the individual, but in families, communities, and cultures. Richard Schwartz and Thomas Hübl offer an accessible roadmap for healing that honors both the psychological and somatic dimensions of trauma. Their collaboration is a gift to the growing field of trauma recovery."

Dr Peter A. Levine
author of *Waking the Tiger* and *Healing Trauma*, developer of Somatic Experiencing®

"Dick Schwartz has been one of my greatest clinical teachers. His Internal Family Systems (IFS) model didn't just change how I practice, it changed how I see people—not as broken or difficult, but as made up of parts, each with a role, each worthy of compassion. In *Releasing Our Burdens*, Dick and Thomas Hübl show us that our pain is inherited, collective, and relational—and so is our healing."

Dr Becky Kennedy
New York Times bestselling author of *Good Inside*

"There's a revelation in these pages that speaks directly to our moment: healing is not only personal. It is collective, ancestral, and spiritual. It is the work of reconnection. For those beginning to understand that our burdens are shared and that healing must be communal, this is a necessary guide. Written with the steady, compassionate wisdom we've come to expect from these practitioners, this book invites us into a journey of reflection, one that gently asks: What am I carrying, and how might I return to the whole?"

Prentis Hemphill
author of *What It Takes to Heal*

"These two genius teachers help you to heal old pain and find new freedom. Their writing is personal and intimate, kind and helpful, and it feels like a master class in transformative practices as well as a sacred journey. They combine deep psychology, practical tools, heart-touching examples, clear seeing of our collective problems, and vast spiritual wisdom. A masterpiece."

Dr Rick Hanson
author of *Buddha's Brain* and *Hardwiring Happiness*

"*Releasing Our Burdens* is not just 'self-help.' It teaches us to find harmony with everyone whose lives touch ours, extending connections not only around us, but backward and forward in time. This is an innovative, bold, and immensely helpful book. Read it to heal yourself, your loved ones, and the entire human community."

Dr Martha Beck
New York Times bestselling author of
Beyond Anxiety and *The Way of Integrity*

Also By Dr Thomas Hübl

*Attuned: Practicing Interdependence to Heal
Our Trauma—and Our World*

*Healing Collective Trauma: A Process for Integrating
Our Intergenerational and Cultural Wounds*

Releasing Our Burdens

A Guide to Healing Individual, Ancestral and Collective Trauma

Dr Richard C. Schwartz
and **Dr Thomas Hübl**

with Fatimah Finney

Vermilion
LONDON

VERMILION

UK | USA | Canada | Ireland | Australia
India | New Zealand | South Africa

Vermilion is part of the Penguin Random House group of companies
whose addresses can be found at global.penguinrandomhouse.com

Penguin Random House UK
One Embassy Gardens, 8 Viaduct Gardens, London SW11 7BW

penguin.co.uk
global.penguinrandomhouse.com

First published in the USA by Sounds True in 2025
This edition published in the UK by Vermilion in 2025

1

Copyright © The Centre for Self Leadership and Thomas Hübl 2025

The moral right of the author has been asserted.

No part of this book may be used or reproduced in any manner for the purpose of training artificial intelligence technologies or systems. In accordance with Article 4(3) of the DSM Directive 2019/790, Penguin Random House expressly reserves this work from the text and data mining exception.

This book is not intended as a substitute for the medical recommendations of physicians, mental health professionals, or other healthcare providers. Rather, it is intended to offer information to help the reader cooperate with physicians, mental health professionals, and health-care providers in a mutual quest for optimal wellbeing. We advise readers to review carefully and understand the ideas presented and to seek the advice of a qualified professional before attempting to use them.

Names and identifying details have been changed to protect the privacy of individuals.

Typeset by Six Red Marbles UK, Thetford, Norfolk

Printed and bound in Great Britain by Clays Ltd, Elcograf S.p.A.

The authorised representative in the EEA is Penguin Random House Ireland,
Morrison Chambers, 32 Nassau Street, Dublin D02 YH68

A CIP catalogue record for this book is available from the British Library

ISBN 9781785046254

Penguin Random House is committed to a sustainable future for our business, our readers and our planet. This book is made from Forest Stewardship Council® certified paper.

Contents

Introduction   1

1   Two Approaches, One Goal   7

2   Trauma, Healing, and Individual Experience   35

3   Trauma and the Collective   61

4   Racism, Social Location, and Trauma
—by Fatimah Finney   83

5   Calling the Ancestors   111

6   Trauma and Spirituality   137

Conclusion   171

Appendix for Therapists   177

Appendix for Group Facilitators   189

About the Authors   197

Introduction

A couple of years ago, we hosted a distance program called "Connect. Restore. Reclaim." with nearly 1,600 participants from all around our lovely planet. The attendees were mental health professionals, coaches, educators, alternative healers, bodyworkers, students, and others seeking to further their professional and personal growth. The topic of the program was trauma, specifically our different yet complementary approaches to healing trauma. *Releasing Our Burdens* is loosely based on the "Connect. Restore. Reclaim." program and includes related, supplementary material. This book is rooted in our desire to work together again to offer something helpful in a world that many of us feel could use all the help it can get.

Why Another Book on Trauma? And Why Now?

It seems like every year sees dozens (if not hundreds) of new books on trauma. In one way, that's strangely good news. For the past couple of decades, trauma has been receiving the attention it's due. On the other hand, the boom in popularity in trauma therapy and trauma studies suggests something far less positive is afoot.

In short, we believe the world and its inhabitants are experiencing a metacrisis. It's not just that we are all suffering from the threats and stress of climate disruption, systemic oppression, the alarming reemergence of fascism, and regional conflicts that continually forewarn us of larger—even nuclear—war. But these and other global issues together create an ecosystem of crisis dynamics with unforeseen and converging risks. Our current metacrisis produces heightened feelings of uncertainty, fear, and division across populations, creating conditions where individual and collective trauma are regularly triggered and intensified.

At the same time, the sudden evolution of artificial intelligence and the increasing speed of information and global technology make it more difficult for our nervous systems to process our trauma and everyday anxieties. Humans have evolved over millions of years to handle episodic stress. We're incredibly adaptive; with a measure of safety, we can integrate external threats and our physiological responses to those threats with relative ease. Unfortunately, we're constantly bombarded with information and the need to keep up and respond in real time. Furthermore, those of us experiencing trauma have to deal with inner stagnations or blockages that make it more challenging for us to adapt. As a result, we experience even more pressure, exhaustion, overwhelm, fragmentation, and polarization.

We also suffer from disconnection—from nature, from hope, from one another, and from ourselves. This disconnection can inhibit our ability to recognize the metacrisis for what it is, causing us to overreact to threats or downplay them, along with the legacy burdens we'll discuss later in the book, and convincing us that other people are the problem and that we alone are responsible for our own healing and safety.

A Different Approach

One singular issue didn't cause our current problems, and one person operating alone has little chance to effect change when facing a metacrisis. We're all in this together, and we need to restore our sense of connection to regain and share our hope of building a more compassionate and sustainable world.

Even though scientists, philosophers, and Indigenous communities have long told us that systems are interrelated and interdependent, most of the world remains under the spell of an individualistic, linear worldview, in which we separate everything into particles. Upon close examination, it's clear to see that everything—the air we breathe, the food we consume, the traumas we believe are ours alone to bear—is affected, influenced, and generated by multiple causes and conditions, which means what we perceive as our individual issues have never been just ours alone.

That's not to say that some issues don't deserve individual focus. It's simply to point out that individual work alone is shortsighted and inadequate. We need to understand that the individual, collective, and ancestral dimensions of trauma are aspects of an interdependent system we are all part of and are all working through. In our view, there's no such thing as individual health. Every one of us is affected physically, psychologically, and spiritually by our ancestral inheritance and the environments and cultures we live in. There are always more forces than just our individual biographies at work.

This is why, as practitioners who have worked with thousands of individuals and groups to support the healing of trauma, we're both focused on collective unburdening and healing. Far too many contemporary approaches to therapy and recovery are still overly entrenched in an individual-based approach without fully incorporating recent developments in family therapy, as well as newer advancements in trauma research. The two of us are committed to expanding the map of healing. We strongly believe the next phase of trauma integration and recovery *must* include attuning to the collective, ancestral, and spiritual lenses in order to foster lasting, authentic, widely accessible, and generative change.

As more and more people commit to healing our individual traumas, we can navigate and reroute the metacrisis by fostering collective resilience and connection. Collective healing work provides a framework for understanding how our collective traumas operate beneath the surface and how they can be addressed through intentional healing processes. One way we do this is by examining the traumas particular to our own cultures (for example, those generated and sustained by systemic racism) with the intention of becoming less inclined to participate in activities that keep that trauma active. As the maxim says, "Hurt people hurt people; healed people heal people." It's our view that both our hurt and capacity for healing depend upon an understanding of our inherent interdependence.

It's true that our collective traumas have shaped our social structures, institutions, and cultural norms, influencing everything from education and healthcare to politics and justice. The good news is that addressing collective trauma can create systemic change and generate ripple effects that lead to healthier, more just social systems. Collective healing work can support leaders, activists, and community organizers in addressing the root causes of systemic issues with conscious, thoughtful approaches that prioritize long-term healing and transformation. In this way, we can all do our part to encourage humanity to reach its full potential and to address our shared metacrisis with more innovative and compassionate responses.

What to Expect from This Book

This book is meant to be accessible, with information that might inspire reflection and further contemplation. What we've assembled here isn't just for therapists, coaches, and health practitioners, but for anyone seeking to understand trauma better, anyone motivated to further their own growth, and anyone desiring to take part in collective approaches to healing. No matter who you are, our intention is that you engage with this book wholeheartedly, deepen your understanding of trauma and interdependence, and expand your capacity for positive energy, connection, and post-traumatic growth.

All of us carry legacy burdens, which are related to ancestral traumas. "Burdens" are ongoing extreme feelings (e.g., shame, terror) and beliefs (e.g., I'm flawed, I'm unlovable) that are carried by parts as a response to past trauma and govern people's lives. Legacy burdens are a specific type of burden that are inherited through family and culture. They can develop from direct interactions with caretakers (e.g., punishment for not behaving in an expected way according to your birth gender), messages received within family or societal culture (e.g., marginalization due to your race or ethnicity), or the epigenetic transfer of intergenerational trauma.

These have a tremendous impact on how we view and relate to the world and do our part in causing the world's problems. Thankfully, we can free ourselves of these burdens and see ourselves, each other, and the world more clearly and with enhanced creativity and compassion. Because our individual, ancestral, and collective traumas are interwoven, we need to increase the map of our awareness and gather the tools and skills necessary to heal.

To that end, this book is meant to serve as an awareness-enhancing vehicle for individual and collective unburdening. We invite you to relate the content to your own experience and ask questions of yourself and the world you live in. Ideally, your reflections will reveal not only what you are most being called to heal, but also where you are being called to do your part in the greater restoration.

This book is a diversified journey through the various dimensions of trauma and healing—individual, ancestral, collective, and spiritual. Throughout this process, we'll offer different approaches to healing and integration, namely personal reflections; meditations and related practices; and transcriptions of sessions with clients and course participants that unpack what our work looks like in real time (and hint at what it might look like for you, as well). We've also included a chapter from our esteemed colleague Fatimah Finney, who was a guest presenter in our course and who graciously contributes her expertise in racial trauma and social location.

Before we dive in, it's a good idea to grab a physical journal or digital device for taking notes so you can keep track of your experiences as you work through the book. We recommend doing so if only to check in with yourself and incorporate what you've discovered in subsequent meditations and practices. Look for questions throughout each chapter for opportunities to use your journal. Like this book, your journal is there to help you dive deeper, integrate your experience, listen more skillfully, and use what you learn along the way for the benefit of all.

1

Two Approaches, One Goal

If you picked up this book (or, as more often happens these days, clicked a link to find out more about it online), chances are you already know a little about who we are. If not, take a quick look at the About the Authors page at the end of the book. All you need to know at this point is that we're both PhDs and leading practitioners with decades of experience helping people recognize and heal from their wounds, and we share a growing emphasis on group work and the importance of ancestral and social influences on trauma.

Throughout this book, we speak from the point of view of "we," using this voice to express our shared experiences and views in a reader-friendly way. Occasionally (especially in this chapter), we'll pull our identities apart for clarification. To that end, you'll note some key terms employed in this chapter, which is meant to pair concepts with their originators (for example, "IFS" with Richard [Dick] and "presence" with Thomas). It's our intention that this chapter provides the foundation for understanding our work, together and apart, and will help you get more out of the material to come.

Thomas Hübl

In the last twenty-five years, I have led individual and mainly large-scale global group work to integrate individual and ancestral trauma. My overall approach is holistic and integrative, and my group process work is specifically rooted in the traditions of mysticism and the science of trauma. My approach in integrating meditation and contemplative practices has helped group participants access transpersonal states of awareness, which in turn empowers them to access larger fields of information and insight. Through my collaborations with scientists and psychologists, I incorporate the latest findings from neurobiology, trauma research, and systems thinking, applying current research to my facilitation of groups. I discuss this at length in the appendices at the end of the book.

In addition to relational and collective healing, I emphasize the cultivation of presence, embodiment, and ancestral healing. Each of these elements requires safe and compassionate spaces as well as a slow and patient process. I sometimes refer to this as "IAC Fluidity," which emphasizes shifting seamlessly among three dimensions of trauma integration (**I**ndividual, **A**ncestral, and **C**ollective), depending on the context. This approach offers a framework to understand how we navigate and integrate layers of experience and relationality. We do this by:

- Engaging in grounding practices and creating inner space to support the integration of our individual wounds

- Becoming aware of the active role our ancestors play in our lives and how they influence our lineage, learning to heal inherited patterns, and reclaiming ancestral wisdom to increase ancestral data flow and relationality

- Expanding our collective awareness to align with larger systems, group intelligence, and the shared consciousness of humanity to facilitate the integration of collective wounds and foster collective post-traumatic learning and maturation

This dynamic interplay enables deeper healing, relational attunement, and the capacity to respond effectively to complex challenges. This approach is particularly relevant for trauma-informed practices and transformational leadership, where engaging multiple layers of awareness is crucial.

We engage in individual, ancestral, and collective healing as one shared system. When we work through this integration process, we can make fluid the frozen parts of ourselves, our ancestors, and our culture. By recognizing the trauma we carry within us, we can recognize—and become part of the healing—of the collective traumas embedded in our societies and nations.

Another emphasis of my approach is that the healer, therapist, or facilitator can take clients only as far as their own maturity and level of integration allow. In doing this sensitive and delicate work, the focus is on relating in the present, and specifically, the resonance between client and therapist. Relational attunement, precision, and offering one's safe and grounded nervous system allow the client to gently move into the possibility of restored and healthy relational experiences. Together, we can restore parts of ourselves that are frozen in time into mutual presence, which ultimately leads to a step-by-step integration of the unintegrated history or past trauma.

I view trauma healing as part of a larger process of spiritual growth and awakening. Practices like meditation and contemplation help us connect to a larger purpose, allowing us to see our trauma in a broader, more interconnected context. To that end, my approach bridges the psychological and the spiritual, as well as the individual and the collective. Ultimately, my intention is to support a process that brings the fragmented parts of the self into a state of flow and connection, fostering a sense of wholeness and integration. Far too often, we try to split ourselves off from the past to try to rid ourselves of what we consider a disturbance. Too many of us walk around thinking things like, *Oh, that's the good part of me* and *That's the bad part of me.* We try to get rid of our nagging thoughts instead of including them in our wonderfully complex wholeness. In my work, I strive to help people restore the aspects of themselves that have been abandoned in the past.

Presence

Every healing process is based on presence. Presence creates safety; presence is contagious; and presence is seeing. When we are present, we are clear about what's happening in a process. It's not trial and error; the present moment is precise. I think, too, that precision is love. When we can connect the most universal to the most specific—the highest states to the most ordinary in life—that's love.

Although I emphasize presence in my work, I also respect the intelligence of the trauma response "not here, not now." Being confused and not being present is intelligence too. As children, confusion, disembodiment, and absencing (the trauma response of splitting space and time to increase our capacity to be present) were often ways out of navigating overwhelming situations, which at the time meant that the smartest thing to do was to disconnect from space and time.

Practice

RELATING TO CONFUSION

I invite you to create a relationship with confusion or overwhelm. Give yourself permission to feel confused or overwhelmed. Whenever you notice that you lack your accustomed sense of clarity, stay with that feeling for a while. Sometimes confusion can give way to stress or agitation. That's okay. Honor whatever comes up. You can say, "Yeah, I'm a little stressed right now, and that's okay." Just bring some attention to it and let that be. When we are overwhelmed, we need some space and a slower pace to give our nervous system time to digest the experience. As adults, we often put a lot of effort into fighting confusion, into regaining a comfortable sense of clarity. Confusion doesn't usually feel safe or helpful, but see what happens when you give it a little space to simply be. Sometimes even a couple of slower breaths and a sense of your physical/emotional experience helps turn the confusion back into relatedness.

Over the long run, confusion and what could be called a habitual lack of presence can lead to difficulties because we need these parts to navigate daily life. Those aspects of ourselves that split off from the rest can become numb, retracted, or disembodied. Whatever the texture of that experience, those parts are no longer in the flow of time. They're frozen somewhere else. Much of my work is about finding ways to "melt" frozen parts and integrate them into the present flow of life.

Integration

Any good development work involves training and integration. We can hone our skills, refine our attunement, and train our bodies, but we can't train our bodies where we're not integrated. By integration, I mean restoring the sense of wholeness that is our birthright as human beings. This is possible by healing the sense of separation that brings about fragmentation and disparate parts. In this healing process, first we need to integrate our life energy to become more whole. After that, we can learn and train. We can ground ourselves deeper in the body, where our sensations become more open and aligned.

Trauma creates a disembodied two-dimensional aspect of us. Integration is actually a reintegration and re-embodiment. This is why we focus on relaxing deep into the body as part of any healing process. People sometimes try to force themselves into grounding, but it's not helpful without integration. We can practice yoga, tai chi, and other grounding practices, but these only go so far without integration.

In a trauma response, we split off the overwhelm and push it into a separate, unconscious space—like a bubble of information isolated from our broader awareness. Through gentle, conscious engagement, we can begin to reintegrate both the defenses and the content held in that bubble. As this material reenters the flow of our experience, it is digested and metabolized. What was once fragmented becomes part of a larger wholeness. The separate bubble dissolves and, in its place, maturity and a more expansive sense of Self emerge.

The Role of the Facilitator

In my process, relational attunement between the therapist (or facilitator) and the client plays a major role in healing and integration. Together, we learn to witness and hold the parts that have been fragmented, or perceived as separate, and we begin to attune to these parts as we hold them in our compassionate awareness. For example, if an aspect of a client's energy is frozen or held in a four-year-old level of development, I match the energy of the client's nervous system to meet that frozen place. As this process unfolds, the client may begin to become aware of the absence of that part. This is what I mean by the presence—and practice—of attunement. We can learn to do this with one another as well.

Much of the learning around inner healing happens by participating directly in the process, by being in the room as an engaged witness and active listener. Besides the knowledge and skills we can acquire, when we're part of healing work, it has a direct transmission into our nervous system. When I'm part of the process, I'm an active participant. That teaches me and encourages me to be attuned and present and see my inner movements as I witness my process. How can I bring the quality of myself to the session? How can I be mindful of what happens for me as I witness?

In this work, the facilitator acts as a co-regulating agent, available to feel and hold the stress of the client or, in a group, participant. This is a key element in de-escalating stress. Just having somebody else in the room who feels you are important. Feeling *felt by another* is crucial.

In my work, we train our nervous systems to follow the internal movements of a client. Personally, I perceive an internal sculpture that sits within the client on an energetic level—a preformed space that holds traumatic energy and stores information in the client. When I get to know that internal sculpture, I learn how much connection the client has to it, as well as how many resources they have. From there, we work step by step as their system allows.

I see the nervous system as a time-travel machine. What this means is that my nervous system has the capacity to be open and integrated, so if I rest in what Dick calls "*Self,*" then actually my nervous system can attune to every developmental level.

When somebody shares a problem or something they want to work on, my nervous system immediately begins tracking the range of ages in which that trauma occurred.

Let's say a forty-year-old presents a problem to me. While they speak, I track where the trauma resides in their body and at which level of development; then, through my precise attunement, I look to generate more space of emotional safety for them. My nervous system starts to ping the holding and defenses in their nervous system until there is a bit of resonance and a response, which leads to a sense of safety. This safety allows their nervous system to slowly open up and come into what I call a "mutual download," meaning their nervous system can download that information step-by-step back into a relationship.

From there, we can digest this information together in a safe relationship and mutual presence, which helps them process the content and begin to integrate it. We can see whenever someone touches their trauma layers because the person cannot stay in open relationship with us. In this state, the relational capacity is compromised, and the stress, emotions, or absence are experienced alone. That process happens at a certain level of age and development, or at a spectrum of ages (complex trauma), when the trauma layers were created. That is why attuned relationship is needed to bring relative safety back to the part that is hurt.

Together, we reflect their growing awareness of this new state so their nervous system can create and strengthen it. Healing is, therefore, a step-by-step movement of encountering the traumatized part and slowly onboarding it into the flow of the essential Self (one's core energy), which is mapped to the central nervous system.

Live Session

Like most of the edited live sessions included in this book, the following is from our "Connect. Restore. Reclaim." program.

I'm including it here because I think it illustrates much of what I just shared: a holistic approach that prioritizes presence, integration, ancestral healing, and the intuitive/attuned role of the facilitator.

Participant: Hi. Thank you for having me.

Thomas: Good to see you. Maybe tell us a bit about yourself so others can get some framing of your situation, and then let me know what you would love to work on.

Participant: I'm from Spain, and both my parents are Spanish, and they were born in the '40s, which is right after the Spanish Civil War. I think they both suffer the consequences from the civil war. My mother and her family went hungry. My father's father fought in the civil war and never ever spoke about it. It's something nobody in the family knows much about. I feel something about that has been passed down through my father. I feel that.

Thomas: When you say, "I feel that," how does that arise in you? What do you feel when you think of your father?

Participant: He suffered a lot from depression and was somewhat bipolar. Every time he had a depressive episode, I felt pulled down with him. I'm getting emotional thinking about it.

Thomas: Give yourself a little space for the emotion. The emotion is very welcome. It really affected you, and we want to give you space.

Participant: His suffering was evident for everyone. I feel he's very, very close. It's been very impactful for me.

Thomas: Maybe we can take a moment with this. When you speak about your father, how does your body feel? How do you feel emotionally?

Participant: I get something in the throat, my cheeks get hotter. Kind of an internal trembling, I guess, in this upper part.

Thomas: Right. Let's, together, feel a bit into the trembling that you feel. There's immediately a trembling, and you feel stress also coming up in your system that pushes the energy up. And maybe you can go to the trembling, if that's possible, and feel the trembling and then soften a bit.

Participant: I can feel also my back softening a little bit.

Thomas: Is the trembling still there?

Participant: Yes, but it's more internal now.

Thomas: Let's go one step deeper and connect to the deeper trembling and do the same. You can soften your sensing a bit so the trembling gets more space. How does that feel?

Participant: I don't know. I feel like there was a lot of space there.

Thomas: Right.

Participant: I don't know how to describe it. Like suddenly, I discovered a lot of space inside.

Thomas: You're saying from a tension, it started to become more spacious?

Participant: Yeah.

Thomas: That's beautiful. What happened with the tension that you had there? It's loosened up? It's still there?

Participant: It has loosened up, yeah.

Thomas: Okay. What's the quality when you see your father in the states he was in? When you look at him, do you feel you can see him? Do you feel you need to look away a bit because it's too much for you? How does that feel?

Participant: It suddenly felt like too much, but at the same time, I felt like I could know how he was feeling. Like I could sense it sometimes, even before he was speaking.

Thomas: Yeah, that's what I feel too. When you speak about it, I feel also that there's almost like a . . . you're very close to him, and you feel a lot about him. Maybe you can tune in a bit with your care for him. How you tried to care for him when you saw him in this state.

Participant: When I think about that, there's a lot of non-understanding. Why he was feeling so sad suddenly, for example.

Thomas: How old is that voice that spoke right now?

Participant: Oh, very young.

Thomas: Bring a little bit of attention to the young part that spoke now, and let it be young. We don't need to change it, but right now, you created an awareness that you're looking at your father from a young place. We consciously allowed it, but we are also conscious of it. It's not an unconscious young part. It's now become a more conscious young part.

Participant: That part got very distressed about it.

Thomas: Okay. Good.

Participant: Yeah, it wasn't understanding, and nobody explained what happened to him.

Thomas: Exactly. You're telling me, "I was very distressed when that happened, and nobody explained it to me, so I didn't have orientation." And see when you say that—and of course, you know I am here—see if you can feel that you've actually told me that right now? Or as you speak, are you feeling more separate and by yourself? Do you have a sense that I hear what you're saying?

Participant: No, I feel closed up.

Thomas: Exactly. I want us to consciously feel the closed-up part. Let it be closed up, but just become aware of how that feels. When you say, "I feel distressed," and when you say, "I feel not oriented. Nobody explained to me what happened," feel in yourself. Very good. We can feel that's gone. We can just feel that.

Participant: Mm-hmm.

Thomas: How you needed to create your own space inside in order to feel more safe within. Then you can see what happens when you feel the closed-up part. If it stays the same, if it starts to shift, if the closed-up part is still as closed up or if something shifted, recognize that.

Participant: I feel like the arousal dropped a little bit, I think.

Thomas: You can again look at the relational dimension, if it's still as closed up, if it's relaxed a bit, if it's still tight. What's your sense?

Participant: There's more space now.

Thomas: Let's go to more space. So there's a bit more space. Maybe there's still a bit of a protection, but now we can feel a new state. A new relational state. When you say, "I feel distressed, and I feel disoriented," it comes to me, and I hear the distress and the disorientation. You can look at how the relationship feels now, and there's a bit more space when the young parts are not isolated anymore inside.

Participant: I kind of shifted to curiosity and to wanting to understand that level of distress.

Thomas: Slowly, we can shift to curiosity and your wish for orientation. That it's not just in you, but it becomes part of the relationship again. You know your curiosity can reach out again and start to be curious and also ask for orientation, and then in a relationship, you can start to grow. How do you feel now? What's happening in here?

Participant: I'm imagining if I was more in contact with my father now or understanding to see if something comes through. But yeah, nothing. I don't know.

Thomas: How do you feel now in your own body? How do you feel now in yourself?

Participant: More spacious, at least down the throat.

Thomas: And emotionally? Is there an emotion present?

Participant: Yes, but it's more calm, I guess.

Thomas: How does the relationship between you and me feel now? Is this open, is it still closed, is it more spacious?

Participant: I think it's more open. I can relate more.

Thomas: I feel that too. Like there's a bit more space in the room to relay. Do you want to go one step further in your exploration?

Participant: Yes.

Thomas: You said something before. Is there anything specific about your ancestors? Because my sense is that it would be good to see how the absence—your grandfather never talking about his experiences in the war—that seems a bit like a hole. Like a hole of information. I think maybe it would be good to go there if that's what you want. To explore that a bit more. Is that good?

Participant: Yeah.

Thomas: Okay. Let's do the same thing as we did with your father. There was a little bit of an opening and more space, so there's a little bit more perspective, and now we're looking at the absence of information from your grandfather. He never talked about it. I would be interested how that lives in your body, when you think about your grandfather being quiet. He was in the civil war, he never talked about it. What kind of feeling does that absence leave in your body?

Participant: The first image that came to me is like a big hole. An empty space.

Thomas: Maybe you and I can just feel together this empty space and feel the absence. Even if there's nothing, we're just both becoming aware of that empty space. We just feel that you don't feel, that there is some kind of emptiness, and we become aware of absence. And then see maybe what arises. If the emotion stays numb or if there is an emotion that starts to appear. If it stays like a hole or anything else.

Participant: No. There's an emotion bubbling up, but I don't know how to describe it. It's like I get emotional.

Thomas: Just let it be there. If it doesn't have a word right now, just feel the emotion that comes up and we'll feel that emotion together. From a hole, it became an emotion. Is this emotion some kind of sadness or grief?

Participant: Yeah, it feels overwhelming. He would hold that for himself. It's sad that he didn't share, but that it's still there.

Thomas: Right. Maybe you and I can share the sadness that comes up and the grief. Maybe we, too, can share this a little bit and have a space that honors the sadness in your family system and the pain that comes with it. We create the space today that honors that grief. How does it feel when, today, we make a space for it?

Participant: Good.

Thomas: Yeah, it feels good. We are honoring together. We are honoring the pain that was never voiced in the system. There is just a recognition, even if it's silent at the beginning. My sense is just by honoring, without even understanding what it means, but just by honoring the unsaid dimension in your family system, something can relax a bit. A little bit of tension can relax. I would like to see if that's true for you. Does it bring a little bit of a grounding?

Participant: Yeah. It's good. It's something that needed to be done.

Thomas: Exactly. The fact that you asked to be here today means there is a wish in your soul or in your being to bring that kind of relief to your system and also let something go. It's beautiful.

Participant: I think that's part of the burden for my father, like he also couldn't express sadness. That's another topic, but of course, it didn't help.

Thomas: That's right. You are the one in the family who has the space and strength to let that breathe and also share it so it becomes part of the collective intelligence, so it's a little bit released from its prison inside. How do you feel right now?

Participant: I feel grateful. Thank you so much. Thank you.

Thomas: You have a very beautiful way to tune in with yourself and listen to your inner world. You have a fine sensitivity, how you relate to yourself. I'm very happy that you're so courageous to show yourself here. It gives everybody a chance to learn something from your process. Maybe others have parents or grandparents that couldn't speak and couldn't relate to what happened to them, and only one or two generations later, like yourself, we find that we can really reflect and bring some healing back into the system. I think that's what you're doing right now. Does this feel good, to leave it here?

Participant: Yes, here feels good.

Thomas: It's lovely to see you. Thank you so much.

> Which aspects of Thomas's approach resonate with you? What is your understanding or experience of presence? Are you aware of any parts of yourself that are stuck or frozen in time?

Richard Schwartz

I started out as a young family therapist with a PhD who wanted to prove that family therapy could change everything. Early on, I was working with clients with eating disorders and found out that most of my original assumptions didn't hold water, so out of frustration, I started experimenting, mostly by asking my clients questions. In the answers that came back, they spoke of having parts that were plaguing them and had a lot of autonomy inside. This was a foreign concept to me. Like most people, I'd been operating on the assumption that everyone had one mind that contained multiple thoughts and emotions, so the idea that there might be multiple entities in my clients felt a little strange. I worried that I might be facing an epidemic of multiple personality disorders or something.

Even so, I kept asking questions and soon discovered that these parts had relationships with other internal parts of my clients, whether polarized or allied, enmeshed or disconnected, much like the families I'd worked with. I began to notice that I had them too, and some of mine were as extreme as theirs. This is how I came to believe in "parts," which other systems might call sub-personalities or ego states. In a way, none of us are all that different from people who are diagnosed with multiple personality disorder, now called dissociative identity disorder (DID). It's just that our parts tend to be less disconnected than theirs. People with DID have usually been so horribly abused that their entire system has been blown apart.

It's the nature of the mind to have parts. We come into the world with them, and every single one of them has value. They all offer resources and talents. Unfortunately, through trauma and attachment injuries, these parts are forced out of their naturally valuable states into roles that can be limiting or damaging in the present moment, even if they were necessary for survival in the past. Thus, parts are often frozen in past trauma scenes, and they carry the extreme beliefs and emotions that entered the system during the trauma (what I call burdens) that organize the way they operate. And parts that have taken on heavy burdens have the power to overwhelm you and make it hard to function in life. Yet, it's important to remember that the extreme role a part plays is not who it really is, and once it unburdens, it will transform into its valuable, natural state.

Exiles and Protectors

There are essentially two common types of roles parts are forced into: exiles and protectors. I'll talk more about the subtypes of protectors shortly. Exiles are hurt parts of us that we've locked away in interior basements and abysses. Generally, we try not to acknowledge these abandoned parts, and we fail to understand what we're locking away with them. Additionally, the parts we exile usually find a way to pull us back down and screw up our life in some way.

PARTS AND RHEUMATOID ARTHRITIS

One major outcome study about Internal Family Systems (IFS) was with rheumatoid arthritis. Thirty patients with moderate to severe rheumatoid arthritis received sixteen IFS sessions and were compared to a control group that received educational sessions. The people in the IFS group got much, much better, with some going into complete remission. In the treatment, we had participants focus on their pain, get curious about it, and ask questions. We usually found there was a part using the pain to either get the patient's attention or sabotage other parts.

The polarization related to a lot of autoimmune problems is between a caretaking part that dominates their lives and other parts that are upset at the caretaker for never letting them take care of themselves. And those parts are the ones using the symptoms. Another polarization I've seen with cancer is between a workaholic part that won't let the person relax and other parts that hate it. Please note that having a medical issue doesn't necessarily mean your parts are behind it. For example, I have a predisposition for asthma and migraines. I'm usually fine, but if I find myself in a dusty room, I'll have an asthma attack. That doesn't have anything to do with my parts. On the other hand, if my parts really want to get a message across, all they have to do is press the asthma or migraine button.

We think that exiling our suffering is how we're supposed to move on from troubling emotions, beliefs, and sensations, especially those associated with trauma. That's a cultural message most of us receive—lock it down, throw away the key, walk away. For those of us with a lot of exiled parts, the world seems dangerous, and we regularly feel vulnerable. For this reason, we also tend to have a lot of protectors. Protectors are simply those parts of us that are trying to keep us safe. Their work involves keeping our suffering exiles contained, and they do so in two ways.

One common strategy of protectors is to manage our life such that we avoid triggers because when exiles are triggered, they can burst out and overwhelm us. These types of protectors are managers. Managers make sure other people don't get close enough to upset us, or they manage our appearance and performance so we avoid critique and receive only accolades. Otherwise, we'd have to face the exiled worthlessness we feel deep down. So, managers are protectors that try to preempt anything that might upset the exiles.

But exiles have a way of breaking through anyway. When that happens, it can feel like a life-or-death emergency, so there's another type of protector called firefighters, who go into action immediately to douse the flames of our exiled emotions. Firefighters aren't concerned about collateral damage or the consequences to our body; they just know they have to put out the flames, no matter what.

When working with trauma, I start by honoring protectors. Protectors are really doing their best to take care of you, so they deserve lots of appreciation. I try to recognize them, find out what parts they're protecting, and then eventually get permission from them to work with those exiles. Healing exiles involves bringing them out of the past and helping them unload their extreme beliefs and emotions. If we do that, parts return to their naturally playful, loving, and creative natures.

Unburdening

IFS is a constraint-releasing process. Parts carry burdens, and those burdens block access to all sorts of useful information. A burden is an extreme belief or emotion that entered our system either from a personal event or by way of inheritance. Legacy burdens, which we'll discuss more later in the book, are those that come from our lineage or culture. These extreme beliefs and emotions attach to our parts and drive them, almost like a virus. One of the primary goals in my work is to uncover burdens, release them, and access more flow.

The Self and Self-Energy

In working with parts and their burdens, I also discovered there's an aspect in each of us called the Self. With and through the Self, my work encourages dialogue with protectors and, eventually, exiles. We want to get to know these parts better, to help them. Instead of going around and around fighting with one part or another (such as the self-critic), we listen to them, befriend them, and find out what we can do to make their lives better. As a therapist or facilitator, it's not me that ends up doing this work; it's the client's Self. One of the distinctive things about IFS is our emphasis on the Self's ability to be the missing caretaker, the missing attachment figure our young parts have needed. This process frees up the protectors because they can see that somebody else is doing the job in a healthy way.

The Self is harder to define than exiles and protectors. People who do this work often describe the Self as who they "really" are underneath the surface of their protective array. Everyone has a Self. Think of it as your core being. It's the *you* that's naturally present when you feel safe, aligned, healthy, and connected. The Self isn't something you have to develop. It's naturally wise, strong, and resourceful.

When we're in Self, we embody Self-energy, which has eight particular "C-word" qualities: curiosity, confidence, calmness, compassion, creativity, courage, clarity, and connectedness.

The Four Goals of IFS

There are lots of practices out there that might help you become more mindful of your parts. Meditation is one of them. You get better at noticing your thoughts and emotions, but too often, your awareness and your Self are sort of standing off to the side. You might become more accepting of your parts over time, but you don't really interact with them much. In IFS, we're interested in going beyond tranquil observation.

IFS has four specific goals in mind:

1. **Unburdening Parts:** We do our best to liberate all parts and transform them to fulfill their original design.

2. **Trusting in the Self's Leadership:** As the Self gets to know the parts and takes on more of a caregiving role, the parts gradually relax into relying on the Self as their leader.

3. **Reharmonizing the System:** The parts that were previously estranged or fighting with one another learn to work together and love one another.

4. **Manifesting Self-Leadership in the World:** This final goal is about bringing our Self-energy to the outside world for the good of all.

IFS in Practice

This is my model of transformation: helping parts leave their extreme states and become who they were designed to be. To do that, we must release their burdens and help them out of the past. And to do *that*, we must access the Self. Accessing the Self is a major part of IFS. Clients with extensive trauma histories are often afraid of the Self. They might know about it, but they are resistant to having it accessed. It can take a lot of negotiation with protector parts to reassure them that accessing the Self is worthy and safe.

A lot of other therapies seem afraid of their clients leaving the "window of tolerance." When a client becomes triggered, the therapists act quickly to ground them (for example, by having them feel their feet on the floor) and return to present awareness. Unfortunately, this often sends an unwelcome message to the parts that are triggered, especially if those parts are exiles who already feel unwanted.

Instead, I relate to the scared parts directly. I say something like, "I see you're really scared. You're welcome here. It's great that you're here. I want to help, and it will be a lot easier for me to help if you pull back just a little bit so the other parts of you can come in and help you too." Most parts are willing to pull back if they trust it's in their best interest to do so, and in that way, they gradually become grounded.

Scared parts take over in the first place because their experience is that they have to totally grab you and not let go because you're probably going to lock them back up again. But separating a little bit doesn't mean getting locked up, and I make sure to tell the parts as much. When they get it, they tend to cooperate.

Let's say there's a hypercritical part in you that you normally try to drown out. In IFS, we'd assume that there's another part who doesn't want that inner critic to speak. Even so, the critic has something to say (often quite a bit) and it's probably going to keep talking until someone (i.e., the Self) pays attention to it. To do that, we'd get the parts that don't want the critic to speak to stand down for a little while. We'd ask them if they could step back just for a little while so we can hear what the critical part wants to say.

In this process, the Self might come forward and express curiosity about the critic, have compassion for it, and act in a clear and calm manner. We find out where and why the critic is stuck in the past. Who is it trying to protect? How old is that little person? How old does it think you are? This is how critics can gradually turn into cheerleaders or wise advisors.

The part that didn't want the critic to speak is a protector, and protectors need attention too. They have healing journeys as well.

> What do you think about Dick's notion that our personalities are made of parts? Are you aware of any exiles or protectors in yourself? What words would you use to describe your true Self?

Embodying Self-Energy as a Therapist and Facilitator

If I can embody a lot of Self-energy, I can help my clients' parts feel safe and help them access their own Self. I literally feel energy vibrating through my body. When they access Self-energy, other people can feel it. Those C-word qualities (compassion, connectedness, and so on) help their protectors feel safe, and it encourages them to access their own Self. My relationship with a client isn't the most important healing element. My Self-energy is simply a means to encourage them to access their own Self, which then becomes the primary healer of their parts. In my work, the client becomes their own primary attachment figure, providing themselves with a sense of emotional security, and I'm a supportive secondary caretaker along for the ride.

Sometimes working with exiles can go fairly fast when I bring in a lot of Self-energy. It took me a long time to be able to do that because I had to do a lot of unburdening in my own parts. Before that, they'd just block my Self-energy and get in the way of the process. Now that they don't so much, people can sense that, and it really helps when working with others.

My main focus is on accessing a lot of my Self, so I'm always checking in with those eight C-word qualities. If those aren't online, I look into getting my parts to open up more space. Basically, I notice how much Self-energy I'm feeling, and I notice how open my heart is. Do I have a big agenda or not? How attentive and compassionate am I? I check all of that before I start, and if I can bring a lot of that Self-energy, it immediately helps the client's protectors relax more.

The main goal is to help these protectors open a lot of space, which then helps the client access a lot of Self because it's contagious. Then, when they're in Self, I help them begin asking their parts questions to get to them, I work to understand where they're stuck in the past, and ultimately, I have them go into those scenes and be with their exiles in the ways they needed at the time. Eventually, we update those parts and bring them back to life in the body in order for the person to enjoy connecting with all the wonderful qualities they didn't have connection to before.

How to Relate with Your Inner Critic

One part people in Western cultures often struggle with is the "inner critic." Typically, we fight with that hypercritical voice inside and try to quiet it, but if we instead get curious about it, find out what it's trying to protect, and honor that, the voice softens quite a bit. So the next time you notice your inner critic, try using a different approach and see if you can get to know it in a fresh way. Here's an exercise to help you do just that.

Practice

RELATING DIRECTLY WITH PROTECTOR PARTS

Take a few minutes to feel into your inner critic or another protective part you're familiar with that you'd like to get to know better. Listen to what it tells you (often repeatedly), but also pay attention to where it's located in or around your body. Notice how you feel toward this part too. For example, most people don't like their inner critic, or maybe they're afraid of it. Some people depend on it.

Whatever thoughts and feelings come up about your protector part, know that they're coming from other parts of you. Ask those parts that are sending you those feelings to just relax a little bit so you can get to know the protector part you chose. Remind them that you're not going to let the inner critic take over; you just want to improve your relationship with it and get to know it differently.

If these parts agree to give you access to the protector, you can start by asking it some nonthreatening, open-ended questions: What does it want you to know about itself? What is it afraid will happen if it doesn't criticize you? What does it need to protect?

Whenever you ask questions of your parts, don't think of the answers. Just let them arise. Whatever the answers are, you'll learn a lot about what the part is trying to protect and how it thinks it must do so. Extend some appreciation for that. Let that part know you recognize its intentions are good. See how it reacts to that appreciation.

Another helpful question to include is to ask how old the part thinks you are. Again, wait for the answer. You're not asking how old *it* is, but how old *you* are. Chances are it thinks you're pretty young—single digits, even—because that's where the part it's protecting suffered a particular trauma. Go ahead and update it with your true age. Notice how it reacts.

Finally, ask this part what it needs from you going forward. What kind of relationship would it like to have with you? How does it need you to show up for it?

When you've spent some time getting to know this part in this way and things start to feel complete, go ahead and thank your inner critic or other protector part for everything it told you and let you know. Make sure to remind it that this won't be the last time you encounter it, and let it know that you're going to follow up with it later on.

As a last step, take a few deep breaths and return to the room and the present moment.

As a concluding note, I encourage you to have ongoing interaction with your parts. After you initially meet them consciously, it's valuable to keep doing so to nurture your relationships with them.

2

Trauma, Healing, and Individual Experience

Before we explore the collective and cross-generational implications of our work, let's unpack what we mean by the terms "trauma" and "healing."

Defining Trauma

There might be as many working definitions of trauma as there are books on the subject. Here are what some of the current thought-leaders on the subject have to say:

- According to **Bessel van der Kolk,** trauma is an event that overwhelms our nervous system, alters how we perceive the world, and results in ongoing feelings of fear and behaviors or states that can make it difficult to function.

- **Janina Fisher** defines trauma as an ongoing felt lack of safety that impacts us mentally and emotionally, originating from a broad range of harmful experiences or enduring conditions.

- In *Trauma: The Invisible Epidemic*, **Paul Conti** likens trauma to the insidiousness of a virus, environmental pollution, or parasites. Trauma is "anything that causes emotional or physical pain and leaves its mark on a person as life moves forward."

What these definitions have in common is an individual focus. There's little doubt that we experience trauma individually, and to that point, we agree that trauma is an event or series of events that negatively affect our inner systems and can make us lose trust in ourselves. As mentioned before, trauma also causes parts of us to become "frozen" at the age when the traumatic event occurred, which means we carry the beliefs and emotions from that time forward, affecting our perceptions and experiences in the present moment. Before these parts of us became stuck in their pain, they were curious, playful, loving, and creative inner children. Trauma burdened them to live under the spell of worthlessness, terror, hopelessness, and shame. If, soon after the trauma, we were able to help those parts unburden, then the event would not have been traumatizing and would not have had such lasting deleterious effect.

The trauma response is ingrained in our nervous systems. Over thousands of generations and through our ancestors, this response has evolved to protect us and help us survive. Traumatic events generate such escalated stress and pain that they become too much to experience, which causes parts of us to shut down. That makes perfect sense in the moment. Unfortunately, after the dangerous or harmful moment is gone, we experience the world with an internal crack, with separation, and with hyper- or hypo-emotional activation. Additionally, the part of our being that's frozen in time is easily triggered and can, therefore, create all sorts of pernicious symptoms until it's finally integrated. Trigger symptoms range from highly charged stress reactions to numbness.

To restate, trauma is an unintegrated part of the past that remains stuck in time, creating patterns of reactivity and limiting our ability to fully engage with the present. Because it's stuck, trauma is a circular energy that generates recurrent patterns, and those patterns don't tend to change or get updated with new information. This is because they can't. As neurologist Sigmund Freud noted, unconscious trauma is subject to "repetition compulsion." Specifically, he observed that those who do not remember their repressed past trauma may tend to repeat it in their present life. What's frozen usually stays frozen, despite adaptability in other aspects or parts of an individual. The same dynamic holds true for larger systems as well: families, work environments, local communities, and cultures as a whole.

Traumatic events for individuals come in various tragic forms: parental neglect, abuse, abandonment, rejection, shaming, bullying, humiliation, traffic accidents, physical attacks, and the loss of beloved relatives, lovers, and companions. Collective and ancestral traumas—the subjects of later chapters—can arise in much the same way, but they're often the result of more encompassing tragedies, like natural disasters, epidemics, wars, genocide, famine, displacement, and systemic oppression.

Why Trauma Is Difficult to Address

This is a topic we'll elaborate on throughout the book. For now, we'll highlight four pervasive factors that often make trauma challenging for us to deal with individually and collectively:

- **Disconnection and Lack of Awareness:** The traumatized parts of us often remain outside the realm of our conscious awareness because they're buried deep within the nervous system. As a result, we may not even realize we carry trauma or that our reactions and behaviors are influenced by unprocessed experiences from our past. Additionally, the nervous system's response to overwhelming experiences can lead protective parts to dissociate. This means we might habitually avoid feeling certain sensations or emotions because they're simply too painful to experience.

- **Isolation and Inadequate Relational Support:** There's a longstanding paradigm that says the mind is a single entity. One of the more insidious effects of this belief is that we too readily pathologize the parts of us that suffer from trauma. Too many of us also suffer from the rugged individualist belief that we should simply toughen up and "move on" from our painful experiences. That only further exiles the hurt, terrified, and shamed parts of us that remain stuck in the past. In contrast to hyper-individualism in the face of personal struggle, humans are relational beings to our core. In truth, our nervous systems co-evolved with others close to us, and we need others to feel safe and to heal. This also means relational ruptures are often the cause of our trauma, and the absence of supportive relationships or safe spaces to process our trauma can significantly hinder recovery.

- **Cultural and Collective Factors:** In cultures marked with a lack of emotional openness and in which trauma is stigmatized, vulnerability can be viewed with mockery or contempt, which can lead us to suppress difficult experiences. When trauma is pathologized, we often see ourselves as weak, dysfunctional, and shameful. When it comes to collective or ancestral trauma, societal silence or denial of certain historical events can keep trauma unprocessed for generations, making it difficult for us to address our personal manifestations of these collective wounds. Additionally, the speed of modern life, with its constant stream of distractions, can prevent us from creating the space we need to integrate our trauma.

- **Trauma Is in the Body:** There's no mental disorder that isn't also a disorder of our bodies, but trauma is uniquely somatic—even the idea of the body-and-mind split is a symptom of a collectively traumatized world. We can't heal our mind and ignore our body or remain disconnected to it at the same time. Our mind too often works as a top-down suppression system, but we can also use our mind to help us breathe in more optimal ways and open up physically and emotionally. Too many psychotherapies are overly focused on getting our thinking parts to figure our problems out, but these efforts don't usually get to the deeper, more limbic places in us. This is why you'll notice that both of us use techniques to circumvent the thinking mind in our work, including focusing on physical sensations (as you'll find in some of the practices we've included in the book, like the one that immediately follows).

Practice

CONNECTING WITH YOUR BODY AND EMOTIONS

Whatever is happening in your life, whatever is reverberating in your body, emotions, and mind, just notice it now and allow it to be there. Take a couple of breaths to connect to the parts of your body that feel lively, energized, and present. Maybe you feel streaming or pulsing sensations. Maybe there's a tingling in your legs or back. Perhaps there's warmth in your hands.

You might also notice numbness in your body. That's okay too. Numbness is an important function, and as such, we invite you to feel, acknowledge, and honor it. Sometimes people say, "I don't feel anything" and discredit that experience, not understanding that *not feeling* is significant too.

Whatever you feel, pay attention to the sensation for a few moments.

When you make inner space for your feelings without trying to push them away, change them, solve them, or heal them, they transform themselves naturally, sometimes giving way to other, deeper feelings. So, whatever comes up, just pay attention and let it breathe.

To help you settle in your body, you can slow down your exhalations as you breathe. Each out-breath can ground you further and encourage your nervous system into its natural relaxation, reflection, and digestion mode. Healing is connected to reflecting. When you start to pay more attention to your inner architecture, you foster more inner space and introspection.

After a few moments of attending to your body and emotions like this, you might begin to notice awareness itself. You're aware of your physical sensations, but you also might notice the part of you that is aware. What's it like? You don't have to think about it. Just notice.

To end this practice, take a few more deep breaths and gradually resume your reading or whatever else you were doing before.

That Which Is Frozen Can (and Will) Melt

No matter the source, nature, or form of stuckness it takes, trauma can feel permanently frozen, as if it were an immutable aspect of our internal structure. The good news is when we integrate our trauma, we reclaim our pliability. The Self and its parts weren't designed to be stuck in the past; they're actually adept at being responsive to the varieties of the present moment. When we're integrated, we experience a flow much larger than the sum of our parts, much like a moving piece of music is more than the assembly of instruments comprising it.

Healing our trauma can feel like melting with the music of a much larger orchestra. Through the integration of space, time, and rhythm, we connect into a more expansive whole. People sometimes refer to this as "ego death," even though there's no part of us that needs to die. Melting isn't death; it's simply an expression of who we've always been. We don't disappear. Even the parts of us that were traumatized and frozen don't disappear. We continue to feel everything—physically, emotionally, and spiritually—albeit in a more conscious, updated, and adaptive manner.

Defining Healing

Healing means that our traumatized parts have become unstuck and that they've melted enough to manifest as valuable aspects of a greater whole. These parts then work together with each other, and they trust in the compassionate leadership of the Self. Healing involves reintegrating fragmented parts, restoring internal connection, and bringing more awareness and presence to our traumas to process and release them in the present.

Healing also means becoming aware of our hidden influences and integrating them through conscious awareness. This process requires both individual practices—meditation, self-inquiry, and embodiment—and collective healing, such as group support, rituals, and dialogue. We can also include whatever leads to embodied presence, supportive relationships, and a willingness to confront difficult emotions. Healing is a process of reconnecting with oneself, others, and the present moment, allowing what has been fragmented to come back into a flow of integration. For this reason, healing requires caring, attuned relationships. Resonating with other nervous systems empowers us to connect to our traumatized parts and integrate them into the present moment.

Every moment of healing results from the unintegrated past finding peace in the present moment. What was stuck in space-time before becomes integrated into the wholeness of a human being, family, or culture, thereby transforming from a non-emergent process (repetition compulsion, for example) to an adaptive, beneficial, and emergent one.

What Parts of Ourselves Need Healing?

Sometimes the answer to that question isn't as obvious as it would seem. When it comes to healing from trauma, here are some signs to look for:

- **Recurring Patterns or Cycles:** If a person finds themselves reacting disproportionately to certain situations or experiences, this can be a sign of unresolved trauma. For example, sudden outbursts of anger, anxiety, or deep sadness that seem out of proportion to the trigger may indicate underlying wounds that have not yet been integrated. Repeated behavioral and relational patterns that feel negative or self-sabotaging can also signify unhealed trauma. This includes continuously attracting similar kinds of relationships or situations that recreate painful dynamics.

- **Disconnection, Lack of Presence, or Numbness:** A sense of being disconnected from oneself, others, or the world can also signal a need for healing. This disconnection often manifests as a lack of emotional engagement, a sense of numbness, or difficulty feeling joy and connection. Frequently dwelling on the past, worrying excessively about the future, or experiencing extended states of hypervigilance or rumination can also indicate that parts of the psyche are still frozen in past events, making it difficult to attend to the here and now.

- **Chronic Tension and Other Physical Symptoms:** Chronic physical tension and fatigue, unexplained aches, or other somatic symptoms that cannot easily be explained by medical conditions can be linked to unresolved trauma. The body holds much of the unprocessed material from the past, which can manifest as physical ailments when not addressed.

- **Feeling Stuck or Blocked in Life:** Beyond repeating detrimental patterns, a pervasive sense of being stuck—whether in a career, creative pursuits, or personal growth—can indicate a need for healing. Trauma can create inner walls or obstacles that block a person's full expression and potential. Rediscovering our agency is an important resource for, and a consequence of, our healing process.

- **Longing for Wholeness or Inner Peace:** A deep, often unspoken sense that something is missing in life can also be an indicator that healing is needed. And a longing for greater peace in one's life should always be investigated.

Live Session

Not all of the previously mentioned symptoms are evident in the session that follows, but see which ones this volunteer might be experiencing or hinting at during his one-on-one IFS session with Dick.

> **Dick:** Thanks for volunteering. We had a chance to connect a little bit beforehand. How are you feeling?
>
> **Participant:** There's anticipation, adrenaline . . . Some active protectors, but yeah. I'm okay.
>
> **Dick:** Was there a place you thought of starting? Was there a protector you wanted to get to know or change?
>
> **Participant:** Something I've been trying to do for years is ground more. I'm finding it really difficult to be embodied, and I live predominantly in my mind. The more I try to settle into being embodied and grounded, there's a lot of hypervigilance and sensitivity, which really, yeah, just takes me away. I just want to try to focus on dropping in more.
>
> **Dick:** It sounds like there have been parts of you that are reluctant to let you feel grounded in your body, and you've been struggling with them, trying to get them to let you do that. Does that sound accurate?
>
> **Participant:** Yeah, sure.

Dick: Do you want to start there, with the parts that try to keep you out of your body?

Participant: Some context first. About five years ago, I got fibromyalgia, so I've been experiencing a lot of discomfort from that.

Dick: That would be another place we could start. I do a lot of work with fibromyalgia and other medical symptoms.

Participant: I think the place that would benefit me more is my knotted-up feeling in my solar plexus. It feels like terror.

Dick: Okay. That terror may be what we call an exile. Generally, before we go there, do you have any fear about going to it?

Participant: No. I'm willing.

Dick: If at any point it seems like it's too much or parts get scared about it, they can interrupt us and we'll negotiate.

Participant: Great.

Dick: Okay, so go ahead and focus on that terror in your solar plexus and tell me when you can sense it.

Participant: I can feel it now.

Dick: As you notice it there, how do you feel toward that part of you that's so scared?

Participant: I reject it.

Dick: Which I can understand because you've got to function, but we're going to ask the part who rejects it to see if it's willing to let us get to know it and maybe help it instead, and see if that one who's rejecting it all the time could give us a little space.

Participant: Okay.

Dick: How do you feel toward it now as you focus on it?

Participant: There's more space there.

Dick: Do you feel open to getting to know it?

Participant: Well, I want to, yeah.

Dick: Let it know that, and ask what it wants you to know about itself, and just wait for an answer to come. Don't think.

Participant: The message is that something's not okay, something's not right.

Dick: Okay. And how do you feel toward it as you get that message?

Participant: I'm more curious toward it.

Dick: Let it know that you're interested in what it means by that and just wait for the answer.

Participant: I'm trying to figure it out. I'm thinking a lot.

Dick: That's a part of you that's afraid to have you continue to talk to this one, so maybe just focus on that one that pops you out to your head and ask what it's afraid would happen. Just wait and see what it says.

Participant: Something about being seen.

Dick: Ask it more about what it's afraid would happen if you were seen, or if this part was seen.

Participant: Being laughed at or mocked.

Dick: So, it's afraid you'd be judged or mocked or shamed for being vulnerable. Is that its fear?

Participant: Yeah.

Dick: Okay. Tell it we're not going to do it until this part feels okay, so it's the boss. Also let it know that I have nothing but admiration for you and your courage to do this. Regardless of what comes from that fear part, I would not be judging you.

Participant: It's really soothed to hear that.

Dick: Also just know that you don't have to disclose what you learn from that scared one if you don't feel comfortable. It's all up to you. Is this part willing to let us go back?

Participant: What's happening is there's just two parts really wanting to, and I just noticed the resistance within that part. But yeah, I want to.

Dick: But does this part give us permission? The one who was worried about judgment?

Participant: Yeah.

Dick: All right. So go back to the terrified one in your gut. How are you feeling toward it now?

Participant: A lot softer.

Dick: Let it know. And after you've let it know, ask it again what it wants you to know about what it's trying to alert you to.

Participant: It's the judgment.

Dick: So, this is a part that carries a lot of terror about judgment. Does that make sense to you, that it would feel that way? That it would carry that?

Participant: Yeah.

Dick: Can you let it know that makes sense? How do you feel toward it as you learn that that's what its fear is about?

Participant: Compassion.

Dick: Let it know that, that you have a lot of compassion for it, and see how it reacts to your compassion now.

Participant: I can feel it moving. Moving out of the way. I feel less . . . It feels like it's dropped more. Moved out of the way.

Dick: Do you want to stay with that, or is there something else coming then?

Participant: I feel a shift. It's relaxed.

Dick: And how does that feel?

Participant: Pretty good.

Dick: This was the part we started with in your solar plexus?

Participant: Yeah.

Dick: Let it know you're grateful that it's relaxing a little bit and that it seems to appreciate your compassion, and if it feels right to you, you could even apologize to it for being hard on it all this time.

Participant: I feel quite a lot of sadness and emotion there.

Dick: Is it okay to feel all that?

Participant: Yeah, totally. And it's because of the hardness.

Dick: So we're just going to apologize to it for being so hard on it. And if it feels right, let it know this is the beginning of a new relationship with it. See how it reacts.

Participant: It likes that.

Dick: Okay. See if there's anything else that it wants you to know for now before we shift.

Participant: It's just scared.

Dick: Yeah.

Participant: I notice just how it dips in and out in intensity, so it relaxes and then comes back a little more, and I feel like it's a forever reassuring practice.

Dick: You can also let it know—and your other parts know—that if we had more time, we could see where it was stuck in the past with this terror and get it out of there and help it unload the fear. Would you be interested in continuing the process later with me or someone else?

Participant: Yeah. I'd love that.

Dick: Let it know that's all possible. What's happening?

Participant: I've been in therapy for six years. I'm feeling a lot of doubt, that it's possible to fully integrate.

Dick: I get that parts of you don't want to get their hopes up, but what I just said is really possible. So thank this part for letting us get to know it and show it compassion, and then, before we stop, let's go to the part that has been hard on it and find that one in or around your body.

Participant: It feels undifferentiated at the moment. It's hard to differentiate different parts. It's sort of a cluster.

Dick: When we started, I asked you how you felt toward this one, the fear. I can't remember your exact words, but it was judgmental, right?

Participant: Yeah.

Dick: That's the part I want to check in with. The one who's been so hard on the fear. Just see if you can find that one. Or I could talk to it directly if that would be easier.

Participant: I feel like I'm with it.

Dick: Ask if it's willing to let you relate to this fear in this compassionate way instead of being so hard on it, and see how it reacts to that idea.

Participant: It doesn't trust me.

Dick: Ask more about that. Doesn't trust you to do it, or doesn't trust that that would be a good practice, or what?

Participant: I think it doesn't trust anything. It doesn't trust me or you.

Dick: Good to know. And given that, we're very grateful that it gave us the space to do this because, yeah, I can imagine that was challenging, given how it doesn't trust anybody, including me and you. How's it reacting now?

Participant: It prefers that language. It feels less aggressive.

Dick: In a minute, we're going to need to stop, but maybe let it know—if this feels right to you—that your goal is to earn its trust, and that might take a long time because it's likely it's been betrayed or hurt many times when it trusted, but that is an intention you have. How does it react?

Participant: It has a longing for that, a real deep longing for that.

Dick: As we wrap up, if I were to give you advice, that would be the next part I would work with. Just focus on that guy and earn his trust and go over all the reasons he doesn't trust you.

Participant: That makes sense.

Dick: Great. Does this feel like a place we can pause?

Participant: Yeah, yeah. It feels . . . That's enough. I really, really appreciate it. I really appreciate it.

This session took place early in the "Connect. Restore. Reclaim." program. The participant wanted to work with a fearful part, which Dick thought might be an exile. Due to the trauma they've experienced, exiles usually have one or more protectors guarding them, so it's best to ask the protectors for permission first. Over the course of the session, Dick could feel the participant's Self-energy, and you'll even note the volunteer mentioning some of those eight C words listed in the previous chapter (e.g., curious and compassionate). Because of that, the protector and exile parts were able to relax a little bit, despite feeling mistrust and fear of judgment. Dick made sure to thank and honor the protector for its hard work—an important step whenever you want to work further with your (or others') exiles.

> What did you notice about the live session with Dick? What resonance did you recognize in your own body? How much of the volunteer's process or internal system resembles your own?

How to Heal

As the participant in the previous session illustrates, healing trauma requires awareness, presence, and a willingness to engage with the deeper layers of our experiences. It also takes a lot of self-compassion and patience. Ideally, we engage the healing process with a multi-layered, Self-energized approach that includes both individual work and relational, collective practices. Key aspects of this process include:

- **Cultivating Inner Awareness and Presence:** Meditation, mindfulness practices, and contemplative exercises are all known for enhancing awareness. Awareness is a critical first step. It's difficult to heal from something we don't know we're suffering from! Being present with our experience, without judgment or the need to fix anything right away, can create a safe internal environment for trauma to be seen and felt.

- **Embodied Practice:** Trauma is stored in the body, so reconnecting with the body is essential for healing. Practices such as somatic experiencing, breathwork, and mindful movement can help release tension and trauma that has become lodged in the body. Grounding practices that bring awareness back to the body can help us stay anchored in the present moment when dealing with intense emotions or memories.

- **Accessing Compassion and Patience:** Trauma can create a sense of urgency and a strong desire for quick fixes. Deep healing involves slowly reintegrating parts of ourselves and allowing the process to unfold at its own pace. There are typically lots of ups and downs along the way, which makes practicing loving-kindness, patience, and compassion critically important.

- **Relational and Collective Healing:** Healing cannot happen in isolation; it requires safe, supportive relationships and collective spaces where we can share and process our experiences. Participating in healing circles, group dialogues, or therapeutic group settings can create a container where we feel seen and heard, allowing deeper layers of trauma to surface and become integrated. We'll explore this aspect of healing more in the chapter to follow.

- **Engaging with Your Ancestors:** Healing, trauma, and ancestry are the subjects of chapter 5. Working with ancestors can involve rituals, family constellations work, visualizations, and creating spaces to honor and grieve the suffering of past generations.

- **Working with a Skilled Guide or Therapist:** As the transcripts of live sessions we've included in the book will hopefully show, an experienced and compassionate guide can provide the support needed to navigate severe or early trauma, difficult emotions, and troubling memories. It's important to find a practitioner who is trauma-informed and capable of fostering a compassionate, non-judgmental space.

- **Integrating Insights into Daily Life:** The more awareness and presence we embody, the more resourced we become. In time, we're better able to practice new ways of relating to others, shift habitual reactions, and bring more kind attention to how our past wounds influence our present actions.

- **Connecting to a Larger Purpose:** Our healing isn't ours alone. Every one of us belongs to a larger process than our individual struggles. Understanding this truth can further transform our personal suffering into greater wisdom, resilience, and unique gifts to offer the world.

> Which aspects of this healing process resonate most with you? Which would you like to have more present in your life? How would you describe your sense of self-compassion and patience when it comes to your healing process?

Overwhelm, Dissociation, and Disembodiment

Although we emphasize cultivating presence and awareness, it's important to understand and make space for seemingly opposite states of mind. Paradoxically, doing so is itself a way of becoming more present and aware.

Often in our healing process, it can be hard to know or say what we feel. Sometimes that's because a part of us is numb or overwhelmed. Instead of struggling to articulate (or, worse, change) what's going on inside of us, we can respect our current state, regardless of what we're feeling. Feeling present and aware is great, but we can also just honor and make space for our emotions when we're not, which can be as simple as saying, "I respect whatever's going on in me. I may not understand it, but I know it's important." The more we approach ourselves in this way, the more curious about ourselves we become and the more we learn to hold ourselves with compassion. It's also a reliable method for melting trauma (unburdening parts) over time and reconnecting certain aspects of our nervous system.

Too many therapists view numbness or disconnection as problematic. One common solution these days is to offer grounding exercises to "fix" that problem, to make it go away. But that part of us is disconnecting for a reason, and it can be far more beneficial to honor and befriend that part. Doing so can teach us how important the part was during the original trauma, which means that part deserves to be seen and honored, not chased away. If we form a less contentious relationship with that part of us, we can let it know that it doesn't have to handle everything on its own, and one of the ways we do that is by updating it with our current age. This doesn't mean that the part isn't important anymore or has to go away; it just means it can trust our Self more with the ongoing tasks of living.

People who have survived abuse often have dissociative parts. That's how many of them survived because that part helped them get out of their bodies when the horror of the abuse was being enacted. Those dissociated parts remain frozen in time at the age when the abuse happened. Grounding ourselves is important, but not at the expense of violating the positive intention of that dissociative part. We need to honor that part of us for saving our life. Updating it relieves it of having to do the same job over and over again, and when we help parts unburden, they naturally become more grounded and we feel much more in our bodies.

We must honor trauma as a hostage in space-time. Frozen parts means frozen data. And trauma cannot be updated until we find a relationship with that freezing. When information is frozen, only the conscious recognition of the separation or the splitting off allows us to develop that relationship. Developing presence is important, and we can meditate or practice mindfulness to foster that, but it's equally as important that we honor the intelligence behind our protector's reaction to leave, retract, or shut down our wounds and vulnerabilities. That wasn't a mistake. It wasn't a personal shortcoming.

Everything we go through is an aspect of our intelligence, albeit sometimes outdated. No matter how unusual or confusing or disappointing it may seem, our experiential state has a function in relationship to our larger complexity. If we can't be present for some reason, instead of viewing it as a shortcoming, we can learn that it's an intelligent part of ourselves (although often young and childlike) that's choosing the best option, especially when it encounters painful situations.

What Does "Healed" Look Like?

With the understanding that healing is best understood as a continuum, here are some possibilities to envision how the healing journey might evolve:

- **Presence and Self-Awareness:** A healed individual is more present in their everyday life. They're better able to inhabit the present moment without being continuously pulled back into past wounds or forward into anxieties about the future. They have developed a deeper awareness of their thoughts, emotions, and bodily sensations. This is because more of them has been retrieved from where it was stuck in the past and lives unburdened in the present.

- **Emotional Fluidity:** Healed people have melted the floes of their trauma such that their various parts work together harmoniously. Their legacy burdens have lessened substantially, and they experience a greater capacity to feel and express a wide range of emotions without being overwhelmed or shutting down. This means being able to stay with uncomfortable feelings, such as sadness or anger, without being consumed by them. The ability to experience joy, love, and compassion is also enhanced.

- **Depolarization:** As they become more Self-led, a healed individual can bring formerly polarized parts to face each other and discuss what they have in common and how they could better live together. In a sense, Self becomes an internal family therapist, making sure each part is respectful and open with the others.

- **Embodiment:** Healed individuals have a strong sense of being at home in their bodies. Burdens take up space and disconnect people from their bodies. As parts unburden, there is more space inside. With this increased spaciousness, there is more room for Self to inhabit their bodies, which allows them to move through life with a sense of grounding and calm. This physical connection helps them process and release stress or tension more easily.

- **Relational Capacity:** Healing brings a greater ability to form healthy, authentic, Self-led relationships with transparent communication, healthy boundaries, and expression of vulnerability without fear of judgment or rejection. This creates deeper intimacy and trust in their interactions. In their families, healed individuals also no longer pass their legacy burdens on to their children.

- **Sense of Purpose and Meaning:** Healed people often feel a connection to a larger sense of purpose or meaning in life. They are able to see beyond their personal needs, and they regularly contribute to the well-being of their communities, using their experiences as a source of wisdom and guidance.

- **Maturity:** Every step of trauma integration leads the healed individual's parts to harmonize with their compassionate, curious, and clear Self. Less overall reactivity and fewer regressive behaviors indicate that they're no longer governed by internal strife and fragmentation.

As individuals with years of experience with the slings and arrows of life, we understand that healing—much like living—is an ongoing process full of unexpected surprises, twists, and not-always-delightful turns. Ideally, we enjoy a sense of fruition from the healing work we've engaged in. The things that once automatically triggered us feel more manageable, for example, and our relationships don't feel as fraught with emotional landmines.

3

Trauma and the Collective

As discussed in the introduction, our approach to trauma healing is interdependent and holistic. In this chapter, we'll take a deeper dive into how our trauma and healing relate to group dynamics, the larger communities we live in, the burdens those communities carry, our particular ancestral connections, and the greater spiritual frame within which all of this plays out.

Interdependence

Regardless of our individual experience—including the pain of feeling alone—we individuals aren't isolated entities. Our thoughts, feelings, and actions are in some measure determined by the families, societies, and eras to which we belong. We are not separate particles; we are interdependent. Yes, there is a *me* and a *you*, but there's also an undeniable *us*.

We cannot, therefore, disconnect our individual trauma and healing from that of the collective. That's not to say that we shouldn't emphasize individual healing. Zooming in on our own particular trauma, internal makeup, and specific modes of healing that work best for us is crucial. That's how we grow in awareness and connect to our true selves. In turn, we can contribute more positively to the collective.

On the other hand, we also need to consider the importance of collective healing, as many of the challenges we face are rooted in shared cultural, societal, or ancestral traumas. Furthermore, when we work together to heal societal divides, historical wounds, and global challenges, we create a supportive environment for individual healing to occur while also ensuring that subsequent generations are less burdened by the traumas we currently face. Individual and collective healing are two sides of the same coin.

Collective Trauma

When a group we identify with is traumatized, both our sense of connection to that collective and our interactions with other members make us vulnerable to taking on the group's collective burdens. A widespread traumatic event affects multiple people in different ways, but it typically shapes the narratives and beliefs a community holds about itself and the world. To some degree, we all grow up "swimming in the waters" of collective trauma, believing without question our community's stories about how the world is. These stories often revolve around themes of victimhood, loss, or existential threat (replacement or subjugation by another group, for example), and they become part of the identity of individuals within those communities. Group members unconsciously absorb the collective stories that influence their sense of self—for example, feeling disconnected or unsafe in a dangerous world. This is how some of us experience the world as more uncaring, cold, or hostile than the evidence might suggest, and this distorted perception can affect how we relate to others, often fostering division and mistrust or perpetuating an inherited "us versus them" mentality.

> Here are a few reasons some of us may be more affected by collective trauma:
>
> - close identification with the group or its collective pain
>
> - personal or intergenerational trauma history
>
> - disconnection to ancestral lineages
>
> - empathic sensitivity
>
> - proximity to traumatic events
>
> - systemic oppression and marginalization
>
> - isolation and lack of community support
>
> - absence of cultural healing practices

Unintegrated group experiences can be so pervasive that they influence the behaviors, emotional responses, and perceptions of subsequent generations, leading to repetitive cross-generational problems like addiction, suicide, and a variety of chronic health issues. In time, these patterns become normalized and spread to the larger society, much like a pandemic.

Unprocessed collective pain also reduces our capacity to experience joy, innovation, and deep presence. This can lead to a sense of stagnation or feeling stuck in life, as the unresolved energy of trauma restricts our ability to tap into our full potential. As discussed earlier, collective trauma can also foster numbness or dissociation as a way to cope with overwhelming experiences. This disconnection can manifest in feeling emotionally distant from others or struggling with intimacy or a sense of isolation even when surrounded by people. It can also weaken the social fabric that holds communities together, which has far-reaching implications for mental health and societal well-being.

We see the repetition compulsion of collective trauma play out in the cyclic nature of wars, intergenerational poverty, and ongoing oppression, so much so that many of our social structures are so influenced by the legacy of collective trauma that they serve to institutionally create even more fragmentation, othering, polarization, and so on. This is why becoming more aware of how shared collective trauma impacts social structures is so paramount.

It is fascinating to consider the parallels between the inner processes of trauma survivors and the internal systems of traumatized countries. If a country tries to "move on" from a history of slavery, oppression, massacre, colonization, and/or ethnic cleansing without any efforts to witness or reconcile the pain of the affected group, that group becomes exiled the same way traumatized parts in individuals are. In both cases, the dominant group of protectors doesn't want to be reminded of the exiles' pain or of what happened to them and, in the case of many countries, what they did to them. The dominant groups in such countries go to great lengths to deny the events or change the narrative around them, just as dominant parts do the same within an individual.

When any system has a lot of exiles, it becomes more rigid and often more polarized. The dominant group spends enormous amounts of energy trying to contain the exiles who seek opportunities to break out, have their stories witnessed, and find justice. The more those efforts are stifled, the more the exiles suffer and the more factions within them look to sabotage or destroy the system. In people, that's called symptoms. In countries, these actions can lead to extreme behavior and violence.

The leaders in the dominant group will then polarize over how to deal with the exiles In people, manager-protectors fight with and try to control firefighter parts. In countries, the left fights with and tries to control the right, and vice versa.

At both levels, Self-leadership is impeded and burdened factions dominate. Common burdens of dominant groups in people and countries include disdain for weakness, heightened individualism and materialism, drive to control or conquer others, and a need for constant distraction. In countries, add the burdens of racism, homophobia, ableism, patriarchy, etc.—all the beliefs that caused exiling in the first place.

These heavy burdens not only block access to the Self-energy within the system, but also to the wisdom and assistance of ancestors and other spiritual guides. As we heal our collective and personal exiles and release the burdens they and the dominant group carry, we release the healing Self-energy within our system and regain access to our resources.

> Our childhood always leaves imprints on us. Take a moment to journal about the culture you grew up in. We've all been born into collective trauma fields. What's yours? How has it affected you? How does it show up in your family, school, and relationships? Write on this topic for a while and see what comes up.

Collective trauma takes various forms—ancestral, spiritual, historic, and so on. What happened with the Holocaust in World War II affected millions of people, creating a shared trauma field that still affects us. It's the same for the nearly 250 years of legal human enslavement in the United States, as well as the institutionalized racism that continues to this day. It's almost like these burdens form clouds around people, countries, and the planet that obscure the sun (Self). When untold numbers of people are brutalized and murdered on such a large scale, it creates a particularly pervasive form of absence. To heal, we need to turn that absence back into presence. This is especially true with ethical transgressions.

COLLECTIVE TRAUMA AND IFS

A traumatized person typically has a host of protectors who act in extreme ways to keep that person from being hurt again. Unfortunately, those parts often create even more trauma as they go about trying to protect the person. We can see similarities in the underlying dynamics that play out in a country. We can examine, for example, many of the conflicts and extremes in politics around the world as reflecting symptoms from past collective and historic traumas. There may also be an element of "active protectors" that can lead to widespread polarization and discord, which usually leads to even more trauma. A country like the US, that's dominated by a culture of rugged individualism, can create more exiles. Exiles prevent the healthy growth of the larger collective because unless you address these cut-off parts that are frozen in time, there's no chance of them being updated. As citizens of these nations, we need to witness these parts in order to heal. Collectively, we need to attend to the original pain before we can move on. Exiles need you to get what happened to them, and they can't totally heal until you do. Rugged individualism runs counter to that, instead telling us to "Suck it up," "Hide that," and "Don't talk about that." In the United States, there's even a growing movement to restrict teaching about slavery in schools. Those who don't want to look at the painful aspects of their collective past are most likely afraid they might be implicated in it.

Live Session with Dick

Last year, I had the opportunity to work with Rachel, an American Jewish activist and one of many IFS therapists who volunteered to work with trauma survivors in the Middle East. Rachel was enrolled in an advanced IFS training led by a skilled therapist, where she was able to begin working with parts of her system that were deeply activated by conflict in the Middle East. I consulted to the group, and in one of those consultations, Rachel volunteered to do a demo with me. Rachel came to our work together carrying parts of her system that questioned whether she was fighting hard enough for her Jewish identity in a world where Jews remain a small minority. She often became blended with an activist part that was dominated by fear and rage and prone to collapsing into extremes whenever someone expressed views that did not align with her perspective. Despite her attempts to stay in Self, she found herself unable to speak "for the part" rather than "from the part."

During an earlier training, Rachel participated in a demo with the trainer and was able to work directly with her activist part. She had the chance to speak for the part in front of the group, and she learned that the part felt enormous pressure to keep the Jewish people alive. This part believed that it needed to hold onto this deep well of fear because it was this fear that kept her people and her religion alive.

With the help of the trainer, Rachel came to see that her part was carrying her ancestors' trauma and that holding onto this fear was not actually keeping her safe. Rachel was able to separate and unblend from her activist part, leading to a "legacy unburdening," a process of releasing inherited trauma from her ancestors.

The trainer invited Rachel to bring her ancestors into their session, and her grandfather and grandmother both came in. Her grandmother, who had lost her family during the Holocaust, appeared to Rachel with a message that changed everything: "My darling, this is not yours. This is my burden. It's not yours." Guided by the trainer, Rachel was able to pass the burden back through the generations until it was released in a symbolic bonfire witnessed by all Jewish souls. Her activist part was initially confused about how to operate without fear, but it learned that it could maintain its values and fight for justice from a place of love rather than fear and anger. The unburdening work also helped her see the legacy burdens we all carry and shift from a position of othering to connection.

Here's a brief excerpt from my session with Rachel, where I asked her about the impact of unburdening the legacy fear from the activist part.

> **Dick:** And then how was the activist part after it did that?
>
> **Rachel:** Confused. I remember it saying, "Well, what if it comes back? And how do I go about operating in this world with my values?" And it was just so beautiful how my trainer explained it: you do it without fear. It sounds so simple, Dick. But it's so not clear, right?
>
> **Dick:** Absolutely.
>
> **Rachel:** It made so much sense because I think I described that it feels like waiting for the next hiccup to have that fear, that anger, and it's not here. It's been three months, and it's still not here.

Dick: Describe more about that change, what that's been like for you and your life.

Rachel: My edge and sarcasm is gone, and I know that people are people. I know people have pain. And I know people are carrying these legacy burdens, and I have other ones that are here with me as well. I would say I'm a work in progress. I know I have less fear. And I don't do this othering. I don't know what happened to that. I know it's not there. I know I can disagree with someone, and it doesn't go to this extreme vitriol or fear.

Dick: That's a huge difference.

Rachel: More than anything what this unburdening opened me up to was more connection to my family. Before, I often felt really cold and lonely in this world. Even though I have this incredible support group, you always still feel alone. But I have my parents and grandparents now, especially my grandmother. And this—all the gifts, the legacy—all showed me this connection of love that was palpable, as much today as it was on the day of my unburdening, that we're together, and if I'm doing some activist protest or something, my family's always with me.

Several weeks later, as part of my consultation with the group of volunteers, I had a chance to do a follow-up session with Rachel. We worked with the remaining parts of her system that still felt protective—one that limited her news consumption to avoid triggering old patterns and another that feared disconnection from her family. Through additional unburdening work, these parts also released their legacy burdens, allowing Rachel to approach the

Israeli-Palestinian conflict with compassion and calm rather than panic and rage. The transformation was remarkable. She found she could disagree with people without falling into extremes or anger. Most significantly, she developed a deeper connection to her ancestors' love rather than just their trauma, allowing her to engage in activism from a place of love rather than fear.

Here's a brief excerpt from the end of that session:

> **Dick:** This part we just unburdened, what does it want to do inside of you now?
>
> **Rachel:** It wants connection to family, to my culture, and it's sort of leaving the rest up to me. If I want to read something, I will be able to read it and know that if it's bad news, it's not going to do me or the culture in.
>
> **Dick:** Yeah, and does the activist part trust now that it doesn't have to protect you as much that way?
>
> **Rachel:** Yes, it trusts.
>
> **Dick:** So, they both trust you more to make those decisions.
>
> **Rachel:** Yeah. I needed this tune-up! God, it's very powerful.
>
> **Dick:** So there's a lot less panic and, with that, probably a lot less rage.
>
> **Rachel:** Yes, and I just want to continue to let this resonate in me. I would say clarity.

Dick: That's great. So, yeah, anything else in there before we come back?

Rachel: It's just remarkable to me how fear and anger really cover up love.

Dick: That's right. This is a great illustration of that.

Rachel: And it never ceases to amaze me how important it is for me and my system to connect to love.

Dick: That's right. Those legacy burdens really block your access to it. So, Rachel, just maybe thank your ancestors and your parts.

Rachel: Thank you. Thank you.

This case illustrates how collective and ancestral burdens can affect our parts and contribute to polarization that perpetuates conflict across generations and between groups. By acting as a compassionate witness to what her ancestors experienced, Rachel was able to unburden their trauma from her system and access greater Self-energy in her life. Her experience is a testament to what is possible when we meet even the most burdened parts of our system with curiosity and compassion and offer hope for systemic healing in a polarized world.

Practice

GROUNDING AND CONNECTING

Take a moment to check in with how you are feeling and note anything that might be coming up in your life right now. Whatever your inner world is looking like in the moment, respect it as it is. Next, with a series of gentle breaths, drop into your body even more. It can help to slow your exhalations as you deepen into this practice. Notice any body sensations you're experiencing in this moment. Where do you experience flow? Can you touch in with any sense of tingling or streaming in your body?

Continue to exhale deeply and ground yourself even more into your body. Feel the ground beneath you as well. Take a moment to tune in with your ancestral resilience. Feel the deep roots of your ancestors. Your ancestry grounds you to the world, to the archeology of our shared world. Now, shift your focus back to your body. What are you feeling there? Notice any sensations, but also the encompassing awareness that holds those sensations.

You can also honor that there are people everywhere doing this practice or practices very much like it. As you move through this book, know that others are reading it too. In this way, all of you are contributing to the collective field. Let's honor that consciously. You're one of many like-minded people with similar intentions, doing your best to heal and help others do the same. People all around the world are attending to their breath, their sensations, their mind, their awareness. You're not alone in this. Set an intention to connect to this larger community, this collective who is oriented toward healing.

Slowly, take a couple of deep breaths and come back to the present moment.

Collective Healing

When one person in a family or community heals, there are ripples—the whole system begins to heal. We are all interdependent, existing and living as one biosphere—and the biosphere wants to heal. Any kind of trauma work we do will benefit the collective, just as our individual nervous systems will orient toward healing if we create the appropriate conditions. That's what this book is about: creating as many positive conditions from various angles as we can, whether it's supporting personal healing, strengthening community ties, cultivating cultural awareness, or engaging in group practices that allow us to better understand and process shared emotional experiences. Committing to somatic awareness work, strengthening ancestral connections, and practicing meditation and mindfulness are also important to develop our ability to stay present and centered in challenging times.

When we talk about groups, we're talking about individuals in relationship. We're talking about a whole field of relationships. In group sessions or retreats, where people come together with the intention to heal, the presence of the collective is instrumental in creating the healing power of these sessions. Even when the focus is on one member of the group, there's often a positive effect that comes from the presence of others. When a group first comes together, for example, at the start of a weeklong retreat, they tend to have less focus or presence.

Through strengthening relationality, relative safety, and a mutual co-sensing of the group, coherence increases, dynamics become more fluid, and the healing effects are accelerated. Another way of saying this is that as groups connect from Self, a collective field of Self-energy forms that is palpable and healing. Once formed, any demo we do with an individual in front of the group is deeper and more healing than would be possible solely in our offices, and the witnessing members of the group report experiencing powerful healings simultaneously.

That's not to say that everyone experiences a group in the same way. Some people have more resonance with the collective, others less. But there's a field of resonance that's almost like groundwater, and everyone in the group has their roots in it. Let's say that groundwater has to do with an identifiable collective trauma like the Holocaust in Europe, colonialism, or slavery in the United States. Whenever that groundwater becomes activated, the roots pick it up, so when we address collective trauma in a large group of people, people resonate or experience similar things almost at the same time.

When we do collective healing work and facilitate the coherence of the field through relational practices, contemplative exercises, sharing, and mutual intention, we might notice the effects immediately. When we actively examine the group's shared trauma, that information automatically activates the group, and within a few seconds, everyone can often feel a fundamental shift in the room. Every collective trauma has its protectors or defense mechanisms, and often they are what become immediately palpable when a collective trauma field gets activated. Whether we call them protectors or defense mechanisms, it's important to honor this dynamic in groups.

If all the pain of the collective trauma were to arise at once, it would be too much for people. These suppressing mechanisms, therefore, have vital roles to play. Take collective blind spots, for example. When our collective awareness has blind spots or there are places in our collective nervous system that are blank or unconscious, it can indicate something going on in the field that's simply too much to handle. So much of what we encounter is overwhelming, be it the rise in mass shootings or the increasing effects of climate disruption. We think we're informed about these things because we watch the news, but in truth, we might often get numbed out or emotionally triggered and steer our awareness elsewhere because it's all simply too much to contend with.

It seems like we are super informed about what's happening to us collectively, but we aren't actually *in*-formed, meaning we're not able to integrate the overwhelm we experience in response to external events with our interior worlds. To collectively heal, we need to raise our collective awareness and also make these protectors and defense mechanisms our allies. Then we can feel the deeper emotions and experiences from the groundwater come up through the participants in the group. If we collectively awaken to our shared cultural trauma—trauma that most of us normalize because we were born into it—then we start to create an awareness that can help us liquefy the tremendous amount of psychological permafrost stored in our world.

What Healed Communities Look Like

Most of us are aware of when our individual lives are going well and when they aren't, when our Self-energy is online and when our protectors, exiles, and defense mechanisms are running the show. It can be a lot easier to perceive individual dis-ease and health than recognize what "healthy" means on a larger scale. Here are a few markers of healthy communities:

- **Collective Presence:** Healed groups cultivate spaces where individuals can come together in a state of mutual respect and awareness to create a shared field of consciousness in which all participants feel seen, heard, and valued. These groups value connection over fragmentation.

- **Openness to Dialogue:** Healed communities can acknowledge the past without being defined by it, allowing for genuine reconciliation and collective learning. They also express themselves with authenticity and truthfulness.

- **Resilience and Adaptability:** The ability to adapt to changing circumstances without falling back into patterns of division, fear, or conflict are hallmarks of healed groups of people. This resilience is a result of collective healing, which enables a community to face adversity with a sense of unity.

- **Cultural Creativity and Flourishing:** This might include the revival of traditions and rituals that were lost due to trauma. It could also look like the emergence of new forms of art, music, and social structures that reflect the community's journey toward healing.

- **Focus on Service:** A healed community looks beyond individual needs to consider the needs of the whole, creating a culture that supports the growth and flourishing of all its members. The group has an expanded capacity for love and compassion, and it actively promotes an environment that fosters the well-being of its members.

- **Mature Relationship with the Collective Past:** Healed groups have integrated the wounds of the past to the best of their abilities. They hold all that came before compassionately without over-identification and the fear of repeating past mistakes and traumas. They own past transgressions and make the appropriate repairs and reconciliations.

To continue the parallels, healed communities are much like healed, Self-led individuals. All parts are valued and related to with care. Parts also feel witnessed; they have been able to share what they went through and unburden. The Self's sense of connectedness and larger purpose leads the person to extend compassion to their inner parts and other people.

> What helpful groups are you a member of? Which friends could you reach out to—even for a five-minute conversation—who leave you feeling loved and supported? Who do you wish you communicated with more often?

How to Heal in Community

As previously mentioned, groups and their constituent individuals are interdependent. What hinders or harms one aspect of that interconnecting web affects everyone else involved, including future generations. The good news is the converse is also true. For this reason, we can always begin by healing ourselves. Our burdens are contagious, but so are our curiosity, clarity, and compassion.

The more healed and integrated we are, the more presence and active listening we can offer others and the more we can help create environments of mutual respect, healing, and connection. Holding positive space for others requires us to embody awareness of our bodies, minds, emotions, relational capacities, and so on. Additionally, our personal healing and presence can serve as a model for others in our communities. Their growth, in turn, benefits the collectives to which we belong. Same as our body, the social body has an inherent self-healing mechanism—a power that developed over millions of years. Our job as community healers is to jump-start and collaborate with the restorative drive of life.

As each of us does that, we bring more and more presence and Self-energy to this planet. As we've noticed in working with large groups, enough people who are committed to an aligned intention to heal can inspire rapid change in the collective.

On the communal level, it's important that we actively take part in group healing experiences and acknowledge our collective trauma. Volunteering and taking on service roles can help create a culture of generosity and mutual respect. Integrating our ancestral trauma (the subject of chapter 5) is also key since our ancestry is our root system into the collective dimension. Creating healthy relational ecosystems, a strong sense of belonging, and resourced spiritual practices are all crucial as well.

Practice

COLLECTIVE LEGACY BURDEN—DICK

The most pernicious legacy burdens in the United States include racism, patriarchy, materialism, and hyper-individualism. In this practice, we'll focus on the latter.

Individualism isn't necessarily a bad thing. It's just that our culture takes it too far. In the US, we're infused with this kind of hypercompetitive, capitalistic brand of individualism that keeps us disconnected. So when you think about this topic—about your life, your family's, your larger community's—what comes up for you?

Too many of us have grown up being told that only the strong survive, that the world is dangerous and competitive, and that we should never show any weakness or vulnerability. Too many of us are so worried about presenting an image to people that will bring us acceptance and approval. Those of us under this spell usually feel some level of disdain for our exiles, which are the most vulnerable parts of us.

Does any of this ring true for you? Are you ever afraid of revealing your true Self to others, fearing that they'll judge or mock you? Do you feel hyperfocused on your appearance, social status, and material belongings? Do you think harshly of your vulnerability and tenderness? Notice what resonates with you. Pay attention to where you feel these things in or around your body.

If you're able to do that, notice how you feel toward the part of you that carries these beliefs or emotions. It may be that you don't like it or, more specifically, you don't like thinking of yourself that way—as insensitive, materialistic, status-seeking, etc. That makes sense. We're all trying to be compassionate and connected, yet most of us carry some hyper-individualization in us.

Next, ask any parts that don't like or are ashamed of those thoughts and emotions to relax a bit so you can learn more about them. This might not be possible, but if it is, then ask that individualistic part of you what it wants you to know about itself. Again, don't think up an answer. Just wait and let it come to you. You can also ask what it's afraid would happen if it didn't hold onto this belief or feeling inside of you.

You can also ask if it knows where it received these beliefs or emotions. When did they come into your system? From whom? Again, don't think or try to figure it out. If nothing comes to you, that's okay. Just wait and see if any answers come up.

You can also ask this part if it likes having to carry this burden of individualism or, if it knew how to, would it like to release or unload it. What does it fear would happen if it wasn't holding onto this belief or feeling?

If it would like to unload the burden, what might it want to give it up to? Light, water, fire, wind, earth, or anything else? When it's ready, it can send the burden off to whatever element it picked. It can send it out of its body or off of its body and let the light, water, fire, or whatever take care of it. If you're able to unload the burden even temporarily, how does this part feel without it? What does it want to do now?

Whenever it feels like the part has felt some witnessing by you, thank all of your parts for whatever role they played in this work. Then slowly start to shift your focus back outside. Sometimes it helps to take deep breaths to end this practice.

It's crucial that we don't confuse *individuation* with hyper-individualism. Personal boundaries are essential, and individuation from others is healthy and extremely important, especially in group contexts. When we individuate from others in the collective, we can still be in tune with the collective space. Individuation doesn't mean division or isolation; it means we can move more freely in shared cultural spaces, be less judgmental toward ourselves and others, experience less fragmentation, and promote harmony instead of polarization. This is how we can have more capacity to contribute to difficult or conflicted areas of our society.

Safety and the Collective

Much of our work involves fostering interpersonal and intrapersonal connections, but making and developing connections in groups is not an equivalent endeavor for all members. For many people, group work can feel unsafe. It's important to recognize and honor that because unspoken and unacknowledged fears, biases, and insecurities will determine the depth to which the collective moves, as well as the experience of its members.

All of us live in collectives, whether we feel like active participants or not. Far too often, our collective lineages have experienced trauma and, therefore, carry legacy burdens, and we can't just wave a magic wand and wish those wounds away. It's crucial that we give voice to the unsaid, honor the pain, hold the fear compassionately, and acknowledge all experiences of the group. Doing that will broaden and benefit our collective healing.

Practice

THE LEGACY BURDEN OF RACISM

Take a few deep breaths and pay attention to what comes up when you think about the legacy burden of racism. This topic is often polarizing, and most of us have burdens around it. Just focus inside and see if you can find a part that's triggered by it.

Regardless of skin color, it's very difficult to grow up in a culture like the US, where the legacy burden of white supremacy abounds, without some of your parts absorbing it. Most of us spend our lives trying to ignore or deny the existence of that inner voice that quickly makes assumptions about people because of their skin color. That approach doesn't eliminate racist beliefs. It just exiles them where they still can have unconscious influence on your choices.

First, focus inside and see if there are parts that are upset at the prospect of acknowledging that you have a part that carries racist beliefs. If so, ask if they are willing to step back and let you work with and possibly unburden that legacy burden.

If they are willing, then focus on the part that gives you racist thoughts at times or prejudges people based on their appearance. Notice where it resides in or around your body. See if you can get curious about it and, if so, ask what it wants you to know about itself and what it's afraid would happen if it didn't do what it does.

In answering that, you'll likely learn either that it's trying to protect parts of you that were hurt by someone of another race or it doesn't know why; it just feels compelled to do it. If it's the former answer, let it know you appreciate that it's trying to protect you and that at some point you will heal those parts so it can unburden the racism. If it's the latter answer, ask if it likes having to carry that legacy burden of racism.

If it says it doesn't like having to carry it, then see where it carries it on its body and, once it points that out, ask if it's ready to give it up. If it's ready, then usually we bring in light to shine on the part so it can release the burden to the light. If it's not ready to give it up, you can continue to work with it on your own until it is, letting it know that now you get that it's not a shameful bundle of internalized racism, but instead a valuable part who got stuck with that legacy burden.

When the time feels right, close the practice by thanking your parts. Remind them that you care about them and you'll check in with them later. Then, when you're ready, take a few more deep breaths and shift your focus back outside.

Collective trauma and legacy burdens are often difficult to release when approached this way, which is why it's so important to bring this approach to traumatized populations. When they aren't recognized or released, parts continue to create the same problems, the same arguments, the same wars. If we're not transforming, it's because we're stuck, and we're likely stuck because we're thinking and acting within a certain cultural bandwidth. It sometimes takes looking at our own culture through a different lens in order to see things afresh and find new ways of thinking and interacting.

> **Every culture produces a trauma shadow. What are the trauma shadows in your society? Who do they affect most? What goes largely unspoken or ignored in your society that affects the collective? How might you use your Self-energy to address your culture's legacy burdens?**

4

Racism, Social Location, and Trauma

by Fatimah Finney

Introducing Fatimah—Dick

Fatimah is one of the most Self-led people I know. She's assisted me in numerous trainings over the years, and she's helped the IFS community become more educated about the issues covered in this chapter, specifically racism, which has become increasingly important as our community becomes more diverse. Fatimah led one of the six sessions of our "Connect. Restore. Reclaim." program, and she's agreed to include much of that material and expand on some of it in writing this chapter.

An Introduction

My name is Fatimah Finney. If you'd like to know more about me and my work, I invite you to check out my website:

healingdifferently.com. For now, I'll introduce myself as an African American, with the lived experience of being a descendant of enslaved Africans in the US, who is racialized as Black. I'm a Muslim woman, and my spiritual lineage is one of God-consciousness. My spirituality heavily influences how I engage with the world. I'm currently able-bodied, married, and a mom of two toddlers with an engaged village of people around me who support me and allow me to do the work I do.

Practice

SOCIAL LOCATION

As we begin explicitly discussing racism and cultural trauma, it's important for us to think about how we show up and how racism burdens and benefits us based on how we're socially located. To do so, I invite you to consider your social location. Wherever you are across the globe and whomever you are as you read these words, take a moment to notice how each aspect of your identity—how you're racialized, your gender, your class, your ability status, your geographic location, your religious or spiritual identity, your sexual identity, etc.—is affected by racism. As you reflect, you may naturally notice how your collective identity is affected by other burdens of oppression. Make space for that too.

Marginalization is a global phenomenon. In your context, what aspects of your identity are marginalized by the rules, laws, and cultural norms of where you are? Notice your physical body. Notice the energy running through you or the absence of it. One of the ways in which racism continues to persist is through the avoidance of talking about it. How can we change something we don't acknowledge is there? In order to navigate within these systems, we've developed ways to cope—denial, avoidance, submission to harm, and so on—in order to survive. Marginalization and all its other names—sexism, ableism, classism, Islamophobia, and other systems of oppression and harmful ideologies—are perpetuated daily across the world, resulting in the repeated, systematic traumatization of families, communities, and nations. Of me and you.

So I want to begin by inviting you to notice *you* as we talk about what has been designed to remain unspoken. By doing so, you can decide what you need to optimize your presence as you read these pages. What will you need when parts of you would rather skip through? How do you keep your feet steady and your heart open to hard truths? Can you be with the pain of being a target of racism or a complicit bystander? If not, can you notice what strategies you use to move away from it?

If you've been using a journal to explore the reflections and practices so far in this book, please continue to use it to track what you feel, without judgment, throughout this chapter. Also, notice the parts of you that tend to think about how this content applies to *other people* before it applies to you. You might hear yourself say, "Oh, I think so-and-so could benefit from hearing this" or "I can't wait to tell other people about this." If thoughts like that show up, take a pause, breathe, and bring your awareness back to you. Commit to learning how this content applies to you first. What ways have you internalized the mandates of these systems of oppression? How have you been silent against those systems to maintain the benefits you receive from them? Have you been working hard to be an exception from your marginalized group?

Whatever you notice and connect with, it's all useful information for how to make the changes toward the collective healing you seek.

Racism, Oppression, and Collective Trauma

Our collective understanding of who we are, what we should do in the world, and how we should do it is largely shaped by the cultural norms and expectations of our social context. Therefore, it's important to highlight the ways in which culture shapes how we feel about the identities we inhabit and dictate the value we hold for those identities. But first, let's define culture.

Culture is essentially how we do life and how we assess the way other people do life. It describes the way things should be done and outlines the meanings we should make about people when they don't behave according to cultural expectation. We must examine the evaluations and meanings we make, consciously and unconsciously, about other people who are different from us.

The relationship between collective healing and oppression is a simple one. Oppression blocks collective healing and fosters collective trauma. In the United States, racism is one of the first threads woven in the fabric of the collective culture here, and as such, it is the tautest. Firmly rooted, racism advocates for the belief that those who are racialized as white are the standard and the preference over any and everyone else who is not racialized as white. To be different from this standard is to be inherently deficient. The Indigenous people of these lands were different from the Europeans who invaded them, and their perceived deficiency deemed them worthy of rape, pillage, and death. Africans were deemed worthy of centuries of brutal enslavement, dehumanization, and lynching due to their darker skin complexion and different cultural practices.

Difference is seen as deficient. And for those who are a target of racism, difference is dangerous within the system of racism. Simultaneously, the more proximity one has to the standard of whiteness, the more safety from harm and disregard one experiences. So where do you fit in here?

As an intercultural competence consultant, much of my work involves assessing how people engage with differences, identifying their underlying fears and biases, and building skills for more successful cross-cultural interactions. It's common for people to subconsciously absorb the cultural norms they've grown up with. As you build awareness about your own cultural programming, you increase your likelihood of making changes to that programming.

> Consider your experience with differences across your lifetime and reflect on these questions:
> - What differences in others were you aware of growing up?
> - How were differences framed in your family of origin? Threatening? Interesting?
> - What differences, if any, are considered better to have? Which are worse?
> - What strategies do you use to navigate differences? Do you avoid them? Do you emphasize similarities?
> - Who taught you what you know to be true about differences? Were the lessons explicit or implicit?

I like to discuss engaging differences because it helps people connect with the heart of the issue when it comes to systems of oppression. More often than I could've predicted, a common comment and inquiry I receive in global audiences goes something like, "We don't have racism like you do in the United States. How does this apply to where I am?" Without hesitation, I typically respond by saying that marginalization is a global phenomenon, and I invite people to think about who in their societies are treated differently and who are relegated to the margins of social concern and preference. I invite you to do the same.

Practice

WHO IS DISADVANTAGED?

In your journal, draw a line down the middle of a blank page. On one side, write THOSE WHO MATTER and label the other side THOSE AT THE MARGINS. This activity is about reflecting on the way things currently are in your context, not how you hope or think they should be. Get as detailed as possible to list the traits and characteristics your culture prefers, as well as those that are diminished or penalized. In the United States, mattering and marginality are inextricably linked to racialization. If that isn't the case in your country, it's important to find out what the pattern of marginalization and oppression is linked to. Think about the people who are systematically, generation after generation, marginalized. Then, take your list to someone who lives where you live but has a different lived experience from you and compare and contrast your list with theirs.

Without knowing anything about what you've listed in this practice, I feel confident that wherever you are on this earth, people with darker skin are at the margins. That's because anti-blackness is also a global phenomenon. Even in societies where there are only Black people, the glorification of whiteness and anything having close proximity to it has far-reaching tentacles that have been slowly suffocating humanity's communities for generations.

Naming Difference, Social Location, and Place-Making

Every cultural context has a status quo. What's yours? Who is deemed the standard and that which all others should aspire to be like? Race in the US was an intentional construct intended to prioritize the needs, livelihoods, and well-being of one group over all others. Today, that priority is given to cisgender, heterosexual men who are racialized as white. I use "racialized" with intention to highlight that these categories are of another human's mind and not divine design. It is one way of understanding people—a dangerous and dehumanizing way—but not the only way. If we are to improve anything about how we relate to each other, understand our differences, and understand ourselves, we must choose a different way of relating to ourselves outside of this racial conditioning. As it stands now, white-centric racialization lumps "people of color"—a diverse group of people with different cultures, languages, lived experiences—into one group, which flattens and minimizes the variety and richness of what each has to offer. This devaluing of difference must be challenged wherever it is encountered.

While sameness and commonality feel safe, naming difference tells the full truth. It challenges the construct of race by acknowledging that who we are doesn't start with how we are racialized. Racialization is something done to us; it is not something that is inherently of us. When I say "us," this includes white people too. Whiteness is also socially constructed and can be socially disregarded. I feel hopeful about this truth. Whiteness has been picked up, cradled, and protected for centuries, and it can be unburdened, exterminated, and eradicated just as well. Who are you beyond whiteness? Beyond blackness? Beyond needing to fit into any race and the inherent sense of othering in the choice?

Understanding one's social location can help bring clarity to these inquiries. Social location recognizes that our experiences are contextual, and it's important and respectful to acknowledge the context we are in. Naming your identities and lived experiences can be a way to challenge social norms and expectations. It invites people into a multidimensional experience of your human experience instead of perpetuating the one-dimensional understanding that racial constructs offer. At the same time, when we understand our own social location, we understand firsthand who we may be catering our work, effort, and energy toward. Sameness feels safe. And without intention, people with power and conferred social priority will perpetuate their own centering and continue to make programs, projects, workplaces, and laws that center them.

Take a brief inventory now of your social location—how you're racialized, your gender, your class, your ability status, your geographic location, your religious or spiritual identity, your language(s), your sexual identity, your citizenship/immigration status, etc.—and write them on a piece of paper. Then, reflect on your workplace. Who are the people you work with? Who are the people you serve? What are their social locations? Are they largely similar to yours or different? For readers who are in positions of power, it's important to notice if your circles are filled with people who are like you, especially regarding race. When you look at the faces at your book clubs, pickup soccer team, school board, or community garden, who's missing? Sometimes we might extend invitations to a more diverse set of people, but they decide not to show up simply because they don't see people like them involved. By engaging differences and meeting them with respect and compassionate curiosity, the repeated patterns of dismissal, disregard, and apathy toward others with a different lived experience can be challenged.

Self-Examination, Parts Examination

We've all been programmed with racism. It's part of the water we swim in, an aspect of the air we breathe. One of the ways we can begin to make real change is by naming the truth of that and examining ourselves thoroughly. One of the things I appreciate about IFS is how it provides a blueprint for people to acknowledge hard truths about themselves from a place of compassion. It offers a way to be with parts that hold racist beliefs (and other troubling beliefs, for that matter) and work through the burdens those parts have been carrying, often not of their choosing.

In addition to IFS therapy, I use the principles of IFS in intercultural competence consultation sessions. In both contexts, my clients have shown me that hard truths are not always easily faced. At the same time, addressing racism is one of the toughest things for people to do. Whether it's working with white people to recognize and tend to their racist parts or working with people of color to recognize their parts that have internalized racism, people tend to have visceral and profound responses when race is addressed head-on. Their heartbeat increases, they dissociate, they get angry, they feel shame, and they cry. And there's relief. The burden of shame exists in both the one who perpetuates racism and the one on the receiving end of it. In order to get to the root of it, it takes offering what can feel counterintuitive.

IFS is based on the belief that everyone has Self, the existence of a profound way of being that recognizes the humanity of all and is motivated to heal. The trauma of racism, exclusion, and death has provoked the parts in those targeted by racism that vigilantly protect against further harm. And rightfully so. Simultaneously, those who perpetuate racism have parts that have become so extreme in their protection of their own shame that these parts have little to no access to their Self, which allows the further perpetuation of harm against others. Trauma and its burdens are passed down from person to person, era to era. When left unacknowledged and unburdened, not only do these beliefs affect our lives, but the next generations inherit them from us. This transmission stops when we all commit to making different choices. Telling the truth to yourself first and foremost is what IFS can offer if your aim is to help eradicate the disease of racism.

In what ways do your parts see difference? Perhaps parts of you want to do the work, feel ready for collective healing, and are on board with eradicating racism. The existence of these parts doesn't negate the existence of other parts that feel differently. Some parts might be aware of their privilege and believe that working to heal the wounds and trauma of racism is the moral thing to do. However, these parts may be polarized with other parts that don't want to let go of the social privileges they receive from racist systems. These parts might say things, like "It's okay if I don't do this part; I'm one of the good ones" or "I don't really have much to do with all that institutionalized racist stuff. My ancestors didn't own slaves. Besides, that was a long time ago" to discourage you on this journey. The truth is you can have parts of you that like the way the world is right now because you benefit from it and other parts that feel uncomfortable with it and want it to change. It's important that you're able to hold both with compassion and curiosity before seeking to change. How ready are you to do that?

Practice

YOUR FAMILY'S LEGACY OF RACISM

I invite you now to write down some of the things you heard your families or friends say in your childhood about Black people (or, if you didn't grow up in the US, whoever your society's racially/culturally marginalized people are). What are some of the words and phrases they used? What comes up when you think about Black people? What did the media convey? What were the narratives? In the US, the narratives about Black people have long been pejorative. They have perpetuated inferiority, dehumanization, and alarmingly one-dimensional portrayals of the Black experience. Just take a moment to write those things down. You do not have to share this with anyone; this is an activity to help you bring awareness to how subtle and overt racism can be.

When you look at your list, think about how those ideas and beliefs show up in your career, whether it is healthcare, business, sports, education . . . anywhere you work with other people, specifically Black people. Consider how the parts of you that believe those things you wrote down influence your behavior and how you interact with all the people you work with.

If we're committed to collective healing, we must become more aware of what we consciously and subconsciously think about other groups of people. We must recognize the parts of us that are convinced that white is better than Black, that tell us that white is fundamentally different from Black. Collective healing requires us all to begin seeing each other on a more level playing field.

"I Thought It Would Be Better by Now"

Notice what parts come up as you read the following experience of the live process participant, who is Black. You may hear some echoes of the ways in which racism and other systems of oppression land and reverberate through her experience. As you witness the work we're doing, track your system. What differences do you notice between this moment of connection between two Black women compared to the live sessions in the previous chapters? What is your relationship with it? Have you been in similar situations? Have you not? Notice what arises in your system, take deep breaths if that helps, write down what comes up, and keep in mind that you can take it to your support systems for later follow-up.

Live Session

Participant: Hello, there. How are you?

Fatimah: I'm doing okay. How are you?

Participant: Well, I'm many ways, as an esteemed ancestor of mine used to say. I'm just grateful for the things you point out, even with you and I both being Black women of African descent in the diaspora, if you will, and looking as different as we look and what that means in our world. I'm grateful for you and the space you're taking up in the world, so thank you.

Fatimah: I want to thank you for your courage. When it feels ready and right for you, I would like to hear where you would like to begin or what parts you would like to work on in our time together.

Participant: Thank you. I am an elder in my community, and I do a lot of national work. I teach and train financial coaches who work primarily with people who are systematically oppressed in many ways, but in addition to race, equity, and financial topics. As I am navigating this work, what I'm noticing is it is becoming more and more challenging for me to hear the things I know my ancestors actually had to use to cope, just to make it through enslavement. I'm also noticing a very persistent theme that causes me great, great pain, and that is this notion that we're continuing to teach our children in the Black community that you've got to be twice as good to get half as much.

What I want to hear your perspective on is how can I, with all the parts of me—the warrior part, the compassionate part, etc.—how can I . . . I don't want our children hearing that anymore. I don't want our children subject to this notion that when they walk out in the world, their being isn't good enough, that they have to assimilate and navigate and do all these things just to be seen. I'm noticing that as a wounded healer—which I believe most of us are—that as I age and as I grapple with my own parts, how do I keep my heart open when I'm so angry and I'm so hurt? The harshness that I watched my grandmother go through, and that I watched my mother go through, and now that I go through, and my son and my grandchildren now . . . I've done a lot of ancestral healing work myself, and I want to be able to hold that wise elder role and acknowledge that there's some things our ancestors did to survive that are no longer serving us. That's where I'm coming from. I know that's a lot.

Fatimah: Thank you for that. Yeah, it's a lot that you're holding, and it's a lot that we do in the world. There are some options we have here with our time today in terms of you connecting with some of those parts you mentioned. I want to invite you to just check in. Having shared all of that with me, seeing which one in this moment you feel more connected to that maybe we can spend some time with. Is it the one that's worried about the impact? Is it the anger, or is it something else?

Participant: My jaw tells me it's the anger. Yeah, let's deal with her. Let's see what we can offer her.

Fatimah: Okay. Before we go to her, just check and see if there are any other parts that have concern with you focusing on her.

Participant: Yeah. Safety. I'm so afraid, so afraid. I thought it would be better by now. I've traveled the world, and Black folks are mistreated every single place on this planet. The darker you are, the harder it is. It doesn't matter where I am in the world. It's the same.

Fatimah: Thank you for speaking for the part that's concerned about safety before going to that anger. Just check and see if there's anything else that needs to be said about that.

Participant: And hurt. Just hurt.

Fatimah: It's hurt too.

Participant: Yeah, yeah. I would imagine the anger shows up because of the hurt.

Fatimah: I think you're onto something.

Participant: Yeah, I might be.

Fatimah: What are you noticing now in your jaw? You said that's where it started. Having said all of that, what are you experiencing?

Participant: The jaw's still kind of tight, and I'm breathing, so I guess that's a good sign.

Fatimah: If it feels right, take in more breath. If breathing is your sign that things are good, allow yourself a little bit more of that goodness. Focus on the anger in whatever way it's showing up now and whatever amount it's showing up and see what else comes along with it.

Participant: I'm not sure. I know these words aren't quite right, but they're the only words I have right now. I feel responsible. Yeah, that's the only word I have right now. There's a part of me I suspect that holds both oppressor and oppressed. I mean, by looking at me, you can see there's a lot of ancestral stuff going on. I don't know that I've named that. I only self-identify as Black, so I don't have any other ancestral notion or connection, but I feel like there's something there that I just haven't done anything with.

Fatimah: Okay. Is this making sense to you as it's coming up that there's . . .

Participant: It makes sense, and it just feels like more hurt. It feels like, "Okay, when is that going to stop?" Does that make sense?

Fatimah: It does make sense to me, and I can appreciate that. I can appreciate the part that wants the hurt to stop and wants the pain to not be there, but just see if, in this moment, if that part is willing to give you a little space so we can continue to be with what's coming up as it is without trying to change it.

Participant: Yeah, let's do that.

Fatimah: So just focus on that knowing. You mentioned the hurt that's there, some of the identity piece, being Black but then also curious about internalized oppression—all of that that was coming up a little while ago. What are you noticing now?

Participant: I'm having more openness. Generally, I feel tight and constricted, and I'm feeling more . . . Even just hearing you say it back, I feel more connected, and the hurt is easing. It feels less penetrating.

Fatimah: How are you feeling toward it as it is becoming less, as it's receding? How are you feeling toward this pain?

Participant: Softer.

Fatimah: Great.

Participant: I'm not sure I used those words before. I don't recall. I don't recall letting the hurt be there.

Fatimah: Take a couple of breaths to just be in the softness, especially because it sounds like this is a new experience. Just allow this softness that you're feeling to radiate, to fill you up head to toe, and see what that's like.

Participant: "What if this could get better without fighting?"

Fatimah: What if?

Participant: What if this could get better without fighting?

Fatimah: That's a proposal that's here because as you get to relate to your system in a different way, more options are open, and you can see if your system would be open to keeping with your mission, but doing it in a way that doesn't burden you with the worry. Would you be interested in that?

Participant: My breathing bell just went off. Okay.

Fatimah: I really want to invite you to just keep being with this. There may be parts that want to move toward something or do something different, but as I'm hearing you say, "I'm not used to this. I don't speak this way," this all sounds important to just make a little bit more space for it.

Participant: Yes.

Fatimah: How are you feeling toward this, to the hurt?

Participant: Gentle. Yeah. I think this may have been the first time I've verbalized feeling both different and belonging and feeling the weight as well as the gentleness. I've done all the things, and this is different than that. Really being with it rather than healing from it, I guess. I think I have worked hard to heal from it, and I think maybe making more space is the practice I need.

Fatimah: That makes a lot of sense to me, that there are parts that have been working to do the job of healing, get it done already perhaps.

Participant: Yeah, it's my job to do that for . . . If I don't do it for me, how am I going to bring it?

Fatimah: Do it for other people.

Participant: If I don't do the work, how am I going to bring it?

Fatimah: Exactly, yeah. Yeah, I respect those parts.

Participant: When my people hurt, when any people hurt, I feel it deeply, and because traditionally, my people . . . I feel that responsibility. I can even feel tightening back up as we . . . Yeah.

Fatimah: I noticed you said that you felt that part coming, that tightness coming back in. Just offer it appreciation because it works hard. I mean, just in the short time of us talking, I know it's doing a lot for you and for your people. Just see if it's willing to give you a little bit of space because you're in a process right now where that part actually gets to relax.

Participant: I don't know which part this is, but it just said, "Well, what's going to happen the next time a Black man's walking down the street and doesn't make it home?" You know what I mean? Even in the making space, even in that part . . .

Fatimah: Yeah, and I get it. I get that part of like, "What? What about the next thing?" Part of being prepared for the next thing is how to use the now most efficiently for you.

Participant: I can feel the resourcing. I can feel that.

Fatimah: I'm wondering if the spaciousness that you have now . . . You mentioned the fear initially. Does it feel possible for you to be with the fear from this place of openness? Just check and see.

Participant: Not yet. I think I'll need to work with this longer because the fear's not just collective. It's not just ancestral. I have Black grandsons, Black men who walk down the street. I'll have to hold it longer.

Fatimah: Hold the fear longer?

Participant: No. I'll have to hold the space and the gentleness.

Fatimah: The space.

Participant: Yeah because right now, it's there, but it's tiny. I'll have to grow that.

Fatimah: Check in and see what's the concern inside of going to the fear? What is it afraid might happen if you did that?

Participant: I'll lose my vigilance.

Fatimah: Then what might happen?

Participant: Then it'll sneak up on me again. Somebody will walk up to me and think I'm not Black and say something crazy. They will say something crazy, and then I'll have to make a decision. Am I going to jail? Am I going to go warrior, or am I going to go space? That's where that safety piece happens. When I walk through this life looking like I look and being who I am, people don't always know, and they say what they really think. Thirty years ago, I thought it'd be better, and it's not.

Fatimah: So this vigilance feels necessary for your grandsons, but also for you. It's for your safety. What's great about this process and the opportunity you'll have with the future work you'll do around IFS is that this isn't about getting rid of anything. That vigilance and its energy and its fierceness can be utilized differently, but it's not about getting rid of anything. Just hearing you speak about that, I'm noticing my own parts, my own vigilance at times, and just knowing that that can be utilized in a way that doesn't feel so heavy inside.

I want to check to see—and this may not feel right for your system and it's okay—if that vigilance is willing. Not to get rid of it. It can still do what it wants to do, but see if it is willing to put the weight that it carries in a container somewhere so it's not in you. It still has access to it but see if it's willing to just put it in a box that it can have the key to. It can know how to open it when it needs it, but it can at least give you some space to maybe feel the spaciousness more readily. Just check and see.

Participant: If it's a pretty box. We can do a pretty box with a key that I hold onto.

Fatimah: In whatever way feels right, do just that. Put that vigilance and maybe anything else that feels useful to the part that it doesn't want to let go of right now, but maybe it can put it in a pretty box with a fabulous key, just to create more space in you.

Participant: I think fear can go with vigilance in the box. Yeah, they can both go in the box.

Fatimah: Great. Do just that, and see if there's anything else. This box can be as big as you need it to be, but anything else that might be worth putting in there.

Participant: Maybe some assumptions. Maybe some assumptions can go in the box. Okay, okay. All right, all right.

Fatimah: How are you feeling now? Do you notice anything in and around your body?

Participant: Lightness. My shoulders are back, not collapsed around my heart, allowing that space to be within.

Fatimah: Again, I'm going to ask you to just be with that lightness and expand it to any degree you need it to. Maybe let it expand from head to toe. Let lightness fill you up right now. Just experience the difference. In a couple of minutes or so, we'll be wrapping up here. I just want to check back in to see what you are noticing in your jawline.

Participant: Jaw is firm but relaxed, not tight, not clenched. The message I got—pretty sure I know where I got it from—is that I don't have to fight with this notion that I started the conversation with. I can model differently, and the modeling is enough, and the being present is enough. Being open is enough.

Fatimah: Yeah.

Participant: I think I can try that. I know I can try.

Fatimah: It makes a lot of sense that you have parts that are externally focused, making sure others are taken care of, and in doing this work—even in this little time we had today—how do you also tend to what's here, what's in you, what's going on within you? Even just recognizing what's inside and how important it is. That vigilance is so important, and it also needs rest.

Participant: I don't think I had that word before, so thank you for that. Vigilance.

Fatimah: There's so much opportunity here for your system and these parts to be liberated in meaningful ways. I try to honor parts in what they're doing, however they're doing them, by offering gratitude. As a close here, I want to just invite you to offer gratitude to the vigilance, to the responsibility, to the fear that showed up as well, in whatever way feels right for you. Just extending that, knowing that all of that is existing with the intent of doing you good. Whenever that feels complete, just let me know.

Participant: Yes, I think it's complete. Thank you.

Fatimah: Well, thank you for your work.

Participant: Thank you.

> Take a moment here to pause and write down the impacts of the participant's work on your own system. Track where you are right now, note what parts came up, and write down anything new that might have been revealed to you. How do you feel about her expressed fears and experiences of oppression?

Racism is so pervasive, yet it works to remain elusive. A Black person who regularly experiences systemic racism in the US rarely has the ability to be present because the next slander, act of prejudice, or threat is looming. Just as the participant asked, "What's going to happen the next time a Black man's walking down the street and doesn't make it home?" That's not a fear we all share equally, but fear is something that most of us can relate to. We all experience anxiety and vigilance, even when the nuances are distinct. People can be vigilant for all sorts of reasons—war, relational trauma, poverty, family abuse—but when you're forced to remain vigilant because the target is the color of your skin, there's little escaping it.

Racism, Individualism, and Collective Healing

Even when we can recognize that certain people are struggling to get ahead in life, certain people are suffering with poor health outcomes generation after generation, and certain people are dying at higher rates, the hyper-individualism that Dick and Thomas have discussed elsewhere in this book raises its head and says, "Well, sure. But it's not *all* of them. I can name several Black people who are rich, successful, happy, etc."

What that selective noticing fails to account for is the overall system. Who suffers most in society? And what messages are we perpetuating that reinforce the erroneous notion that it's all their fault?

In truth, we're all interconnected. I'm connected to you, and you're connected to me. What you're going through in life is somehow related to what I'm going through. This connection can be a lot easier to feel in times of crisis—think of any tragedy in your country that brought diverse people together for a brief moment in time—but we're not just connected when there's a forest fire, tornado, earthquake, flood, or murderous attack on civilians. We're connected right now. We're always connected.

Recognizing the truth of interconnection promotes collective healing. But the countercurrent is strong. Every day we're bombarded with the hyper-individualist message that we're all on our own, that no one is coming to save us, that you're over there in that box and I'm over here in mine, so the best thing any of us can do is take care of ourselves, prioritize our individual lives, and let others do the same. And, of course, if they don't, it's their fault.

These legacies of competition, dominance, hierarchy, scarcity, and conquering have fooled us all. And the legacy of power hoarding has fooled us into thinking that if we stand on top of someone else, nothing about their suffering is going to impact us. That sort of insidious, erroneous belief can only continue when we don't examine it. Furthermore, the same harmful messages targeted at me can be ones I absorb and hold toward myself and others. As a target of racism, I've had to check the ways in which I've internalized and projected some of these beliefs on myself and others like me.

When I first started out as a therapist, I often had to encounter some difficult beliefs I carried about poverty, specifically Black people in poverty. I'd think, *Why are they like that?* and whatever answers that came were invariably from cultural beliefs that problems are personal and that the greater context is one of opportunity waiting for those who work for it. The American Dream. But this is a lie. Problems have personal impact, sure, but they are both personally and socially created. Rather than asking, "Why are they like that?," I shifted to asking, "What happened to them?" and, more importantly, "What happened to us?" because what affected them also affected me. Racism suggests that the condition of Black people in the US is all behavioral. "If Black people would just do _____, they'd have all the privileges white people do." When you don't have context for how a system was designed to produce the results it produces, it invites further harm and dehumanization. If Black people weren't systematically disenfranchised, disempowered, and underresourced, they'd be able to be free and live to their fullest potential. I still have to affirm, as I write these words, that what I have to offer is as valuable, if not more, than my coauthors

The more we examine and unburden our rooted beliefs about self and others, our lens becomes clear. We can see through the lies of these legacies of oppression and understand that there's enough for all of us. We can be resources for each other and know that our humanness is enough.

> **What are your habitual ways of distancing yourself from others, especially those who look different than you? How might that keep you safe? How might that sense of safety be an illusion?**

The walls between us are largely of our own making, and we need to do our part in knocking them down. At some point, what happens in the next box over is going to spill over into your box, your neighborhood, your community. In acknowledging this, we must say to ourselves, "Rather than waiting for the next murder or mass shooting, how can I step up and do something about it?" A new future is possible. If nothing else, you can begin by seeing through the lie that seeks to convince you that other people's suffering doesn't have anything to do with you.

Doing the Work

Hopefully, some of this chapter has resonated with you. You might also be experiencing some confusion as to how this material about racism, social location, and collective healing connects to you. If that's the case, your work going forward could be to figure out how it does involve you. And if you're on board with the impacts of racism, the next step is to continue to examine your parts and work with any internal oppressors you find. How does racism still show up in the work you do?

As much as we can become personally unburdened, we still live in a world that is heavily burdened with racism, so even when you do your work, there remains a powerful force that is intent on keeping racism going and countering whatever collective healing we accomplish. It's not hard to see that at play in the US today, where it can feel like more burdens are being created by the powers-that-be daily. That's understandably daunting for parts of us that want quick solutions and complete eradication in our lifetime.

We might not see the results we want in this lifetime or generation. Considering that, how do we persist? How can we continue to strive for what's right? How can we keep coming back to ourselves and our part in this larger picture? Examining ourselves, taking accountability, and naming truth is always a step we can return to. If we can't do that, we'll invariably go back to committing microaggressions, making hiring decisions that perpetuate racism, believing that we're all on our own, and living with the idea that other people's suffering is the result of their own shortcomings.

If we want a different world, we must make different choices. And we must choose community and connection to each other. While we are more digitally connected, our hearts are increasingly distant as the digital world distorts our understanding of who we are. For collective healing, we must commit to a daily practice of shifting the narrative, changing how we engage across difference, and challenging the status quo. Those of you with privileged identities have undeniable social power. Instead of feeling ashamed about that or not acknowledging it, you can choose to use it for the good of all of us. Power isn't worth much unless we claim it. If you truly want to be anti-racist, look for ways to leverage your power in service to the collective.

Unburdening as an Ongoing Process

Unburdening is not a point of completion; it's a beginning—a start to a new relationship with ourselves that is not held together by previous burdens. In my experience with IFS, there's no end to the process; there's only deepening. That's especially helpful to remember when we think about our activism in a world that seems committed to the ongoing trauma and burdens of racism. We learn as we go along, we create more space, we foster our connections, and we make the ongoing work more sustainable for ourselves and others.

Personally, when I experience unburdenings in IFS or have extended periods of being Self-led, my range of options and choices begins to feel far more expansive than when I'm playing small and operating from a place of fear and overwhelm. When I bring those eight C qualities of Self forward (calmness, clarity, compassion, confidence, connectedness, courage, creativity, and curiosity), it looks wildly different from when I'm operating from a place of inferiority, internalized oppression, and hyper-individualization.

When I'm able to release myself from so much of what was never mine to begin with—racism, patriarchy, Islamophobia—I have more access to my inherent gifts, I can stand up for justice with clarity and courage, and I can connect more readily to others who need my encouragement and support. But when I'm moving with internal racism, feelings of inferiority, or dependency on whiteness for my value, I perpetuate the same ideologies and become a tool of strengthening the system that my heart seeks to dismantle. My awareness of this and of any fears that persist offers me the opportunity to make a different choice. I still live in the US, which is still a racist society. Fear is a fact of my existence in this context, but the fear isn't failure; it can be fuel. So my daily practice is to question myself: How will I show up, meet that truth, and do my part to change it anyway? How will you?

Homework and Getting Support

If you're anything like me, when you put down this book, it will be hard to remember what you've absorbed when life is trying to pull you in a hundred different directions at once. So before you re-enter your daily routine, I want to offer this final practice.

Practice

INVENTORY AND INTENTIONS

Take an honest inventory about what came up for you as you read this chapter. Use whatever notes you've already taken and those you can jot down now as a lighthouse to show you where you need to go. Set an intention to review your journal and apply your notes in your therapy sessions, conversations, and work in the world. Share this book, set up an accountability group, or establish support for yourself and others. Remember that you're not in this alone.

5

Calling the Ancestors

We don't often recognize how the body is the living record of our evolution. Our bodies are much older than our birth certificates and passports tell us. In fact, they're millions and millions of years old and packed with embodied wisdom. Anatomically, our nervous system isn't ours alone. Yes, our nervous system has personal aspects that house the personal data of this life's journey, but it is largely ancestral, and that means we can tune into ancestral information.

In chapter 3, we discussed how we're affected by collective legacy burdens and trauma fields and how we can also tune into collective information. Most of us have trouble accessing it, but it's more than possible to extract all that beneficial information from our genetic hard drive and activate a greater, intergenerational intelligence. Together, with our ancestors, we have access to all the intelligence we need. Our intergenerational connections and relationships are like a data flow in our bodies and lives. If there is a lot of trauma or broken relationships, there is also less data, less intelligence, and less resilience that can flow. If the flow is open, important information can stream in. But if it's fragmented, we're probably dealing with the disembodied parts of our ancestors.

Not all cultures suffer from hyper-individualization. Numerous Indigenous and mystical traditions work with other sources of information, including ancestral information, all the time. Most of us in the West haven't been trained to do so, but anyone can do it. All of us have the inner "hardware and software" required to connect with our ancestors, which can become an experiment in relating to them as fields of energy. All that integrated history isn't behind us; it's in us right now. Without the thousands of generations of ancestors who preceded us, we couldn't do anything we currently do intellectually, emotionally, technologically, or otherwise. The point is we have so much information we can call on, tune in with, feel, sense, and know. We're not just a separate person in a separate box living a separate life. Every one of us is incredibly interconnected.

Who They Are and Why They Matter

When we talk about our ancestors, we're mostly referring to direct relatives who've passed away. We don't typically think of older living family members (our grandparents, for example) as our ancestors while they're still alive. So, by ancestors, we're primarily referring to the people of previous generations whose genetic material and life experiences we've inherited. Secondarily, our ancestors can include influential extended family members and people outside of our bloodline, like adoptive parents and people who were instrumental in shaping our collective atmosphere and communities. Sometimes these people include religious leaders, philosophers, and significant historical figures whose teachings and actions continue to affect our worldviews and ways of life.

The impact of past generations is deeply embedded in our physical, emotional, and psychological makeup, even if we are not consciously aware of it. Here are some of the ways our ancestors continue to affect our experience in the present:

- **Unprocessed Stories and Memories:** Many of the influences from our ancestors remain hidden in the unconscious. These influences might manifest as unexplained fears, repetitive life patterns, or emotions that seem out of proportion to present circumstances. These patterns often point to unresolved experiences from previous generations that have been "frozen" in time and passed down as an unspoken legacy.

- **Dreams, Intuition, and Inner Knowledge:** Ancestral influences can sometimes show up in more subtle ways, such as through dreams or intuitive feelings that seem to connect us to the experiences of past generations. These can be seen as ways that the body and mind attempt to bring unprocessed ancestral material to conscious awareness, seeking healing and integration.

- **Burdens and Gifts from the Past:** Ancestors leave both burdens and gifts. Burdens are the unprocessed traumas, detrimental patterns, and extreme beliefs, emotions, and energies that weigh down descendants. Gifts include resilience, wisdom, and cultural practices that can be sources of strength. Recognizing both aspects allows individuals to honor their lineage while discerning what needs to be healed or transformed.

- **Biological and Epigenetic Transmission:** Epigenetics research suggests that trauma can leave biological epigenetic changes in our genes, potentially affecting how stress and emotional pain are processed by descendants. This means traumatic experiences can alter how genes are expressed, leading to heightened stress responses or vulnerability to certain conditions in future generations.

> In your list of ancestors, which ones are you most curious about encountering more? Which are you tentative or fearful about? What burdens and gifts have your ancestors passed down to you?

Intergenerational Trauma

When trauma remains unresolved in a family or community, it gets frozen in time, causing its burdens to be continuously passed down through generations in basically the same form until somebody decides to do something about it. Over hundreds and thousands of generations, trauma-based beliefs and emotions are invariably passed down, but so is healing and many other qualities of resilience and strength. It may be easier to notice the unhealthy behaviors we've inherited, but we also inherit many positive aspects we can tap into as a resource or power for healing. In fact, it's the only reason our bodies know how to heal in the first place.

That said, if our ancestors experienced intense suffering from war, displacement, or abuse without being able to process it fully, the emotional and psychological impact of that trauma can be inherited by subsequent generations in predictable ways. If a previous generation dealt with loss or trauma by becoming emotionally distant, for example, this pattern may be unconsciously adopted by descendants, even if the original cause of that behavior is no longer present. Every attachment trauma we experience occurs in the ecosystem of ancestral transmission. Again, we can't separate our individual traumas; they're interdependent with all that came before us.

For example, many of our ancestors experienced World War II and other mass conflicts and tragedies directly. The trauma they experienced wasn't fully healed in their lifetimes, so it was passed down to our parents, who passed it down to us in turn. That means we have intergenerational trauma transmission, which is disembodied information passed on over generations.

Every new generation is born from the ghosts of former generations. And like ghosts, traumatic information is disembodied. Whatever is disembodied and not reintegrated in one generation is what the next generation is born into, born with. And we all have been born into the aftermath of generations that experienced violence, slavery, racism, genocide, colonialism, gender violence, and other forms of oppression. All of that makes up the field we were born into.

Isabelle Mansuy is a professor in neuroepigenetics at the University of Zurich who has published epigenetic studies on mice models. Through her work, she's shown how trauma can be transmitted over multiple generations, and that epigenetic information can be transformed through therapy. It's hard to say right now how extensively this data applies to humans, but there are some impactful correlations. What it suggests is that all the stuff we carry with us from our upbringing—including ancestral trauma—can be integrated. This bears out in the work we do with individuals and groups.

Most ancestral trauma is created through inappropriate relationships and human rights transgressions. In all cases, fundamental ethics are violated, and the foundational compass of what's right and good has been hurt. And it's been hurt both in those who are directly traumatized and those who committed the transgression. We must heal these deep ethical roots along with the parts of our ancestors who were traumatized, as well as the parts of our ancestors who enacted the trauma.

It's complex, difficult work. We need to develop relationships with all aspects of it, step by step. This requires curious exploration and a willingness to respond authentically. Even if we weren't directly involved with committing the crimes and wounds of the past, we're still dealing with the aftereffects. Developing relationships with all involved parts is how we effect change. Instead of distancing ourselves from the past, we can instead choose something new, something different. In that way, we can release ourselves and others from the struggles of the past. Life entails self-healing, but we must do something in order to jump-start it.

Sometimes awareness is enough to promote this integration. Other situations require an acknowledgment of the traumatic past event(s) for an ethical restoration to occur. Response-ability means the ability to respond and be in relation with the transgressions of our ancestors. That is often challenging, but necessary. It does not mean that the current generation committed the past transgressions, but it does mean that they need to be in a felt relation with them and acknowledge the past in order to heal. In groups, we often work with internal sensations that arise when we tune in with certain aspects. For example, when fears come up and we are able to witness them together—and when we expand our mutual awareness to our parents and grandparents as well as other ancestors—we're opening space-time in reverse and creating a witnessing space. In that space, we can allow the trauma to arise, relax, and ground so we can integrate it. On the individual and group level, our nervous systems relax and regulate. The disembodied information becomes embodied, which makes a return to peace possible.

Perhaps we can't totally alter the past, but we *can* release the residue of the past. And since the past lives in our bodies, we have the ability to unfreeze channels of data, connection, and interdependence. The future has the power to impact the past too. In this way, we don't know what futures are impacting us now. What higher future is supporting us in our healing process? If it works in one direction, why can't it work in all directions?

Working with Ancestral Burdens

When we can see our ancestors, and our ancestors can see us, that's presence. Seeing is presence. In order not to see our ancestors and their trauma clearly, we have to look away or cover things up. Unburdening those covers allows us to see with clarity and compassion. Sometimes that involves the difficult work of acknowledging the actions of our ancestors, perhaps even actions that hurt the world and other people.

Getting to know our ancestors is a lot like getting to know our parts. The more we do it with Self-energy, the more available they become and the more they begin to trust us with their gifts and wisdom. Most of us carry burdens from our family lineage, but also from our ethnic group and the legacy burdens everyone suffers from in any given culture. Some parts carry these burdens more than others, and sometimes parts take burdens on willfully, for example, from parents for the sake of self-protection. When parents can't handle the legacy burdens they inherited from their parents, young parts take them on (say, in the form of a parent's anger or sadness) in an effort to feel safer.

When we heal personal burdens that aren't ancestral, it's typical for a part to stick around until it feels witnessed, until it feels like you get what happened earlier in your life to create that burdening. It's not the same when we work with legacy burdens. Usually when a part recognizes that it received the burden from elsewhere, it gives the burden up easily. That's not always the case, of course. Sometimes ancestral trauma and suffering do need to be witnessed, and when that doesn't happen, it keeps going and going.

One common way that a part will embody legacy burdens is by becoming hypercritical. Often our internal critics carry the energy of critical parents, who received that energy from their parents, who inherited it from theirs, and so on. Hypercriticism is often a legacy burden that's passed down through generations, which helps explain why so many of us struggle with it. When it comes to ancestral burdens like that, individual healing work—even with a talented therapist—regularly falls short. As we've said elsewhere, we need to expand the map and approach our healing from different angles.

Practice

WORKING WITH LEGACY BURDENS

Shift your focus inside and notice whatever thoughts, emotions, sensations, and impulses are there. As you notice, see if there's enough separation to also pay attention to how you feel about whatever comes up. All of these thoughts, sensations, and so on are emanating from different parts of you, parts that don't often receive the attention they seek from you.

Let those parts know that, in this practice and others to come, you're going to attend to them more than usual because you want to get to know them, even the ones that seem to create problems for you. You want to know all of them, even help them if you can. As you're telling them all this, notice how they react.

After doing this practice for a little bit, you can also update them about the version of you speaking to them. You can tell them that you're not a child anymore, that you're an adult of whatever age you are now, and that you therefore have way more capacity than you did when you were younger. That translates into more capacity to help them. See how they react to this news. You don't have to do anything about it, but some parts might push back or even resist your offer to extend compassion or help other parts. Just notice what reactions come up in this.

Now, ask if any of them carry energy, beliefs, or emotions that don't come from your life specifically. That is, ask if the energy, belief, emotion, or whatever it is comes from other people. In this case, from ancestors. As before, do your best not to think about the answers to these questions, but feel into them. Just wait and see if anything arises in response.

You very well might not receive an answer, but sometimes a part will speak up and delineate what comes from your life and what originated in the lives of your family and other predecessors. If a part does answer, be sure to thank it and inform it that you'll check in with it again. Also let it know that you want to help it with some of the burdens it carries from ancestral trauma. It works so hard to carry those legacy burdens around, and you want to help it with that if you can.

Whenever it feels right, thank your parts for anything they've shared. Remind them that this is just the beginning of a new relationship and you plan on checking in with them again soon. Then, slowly shift your focus back outside. It can help to take some deep breaths as you do that.

The Benefits of Unburdening Our Ancestors

It's not that our ancestors wanted us to carry their burdens in the first place. Most of them would never choose to pass them on. We have the opportunity in our lifetimes to address and release the pain that our ancestors could not process in theirs. This process of making the unconscious conscious can lead to transformative resolutions that reach back through the generational line. When we heal, we shift stuck patterns, breaking apart the cycle of trauma so it isn't transmitted to future generations. We can honor our ancestors and the past while creating a new trajectory for the future. Through this process, we can develop compassion and gratitude for ancestors where previously there may have been only pain and resentment.

As we do our part to unburden our ancestors, we develop more access to them, which means they have more ability to help us in our lives today. Some of the ways their unburdened presence can assist us include:

- insight into the deeper workings of human life, trauma, resilience, and the interconnected nature of our existence

- tried-and-true wisdom to guide our decisions and life direction

- strength and adaptability through increased familiarity with what our ancestors survived and how they did so

- enhanced sense of meaning as we experience inevitable adversity and suffering

- an alignment with others—past, present, and future—that promotes greater harmony with all of life

Calling the Ancestors

If you invite ancestors into your life, they'll find a way to show up. They might not always be so obvious about it, but in one way or another, you'll get a real hint about who they are and what they experienced. Calling the ancestors into our lives can be as simple as acknowledging them and recognizing their ongoing influence in our lives. More specific practices include:

- asking living family members about past generations and reflecting on the stories and experiences we discover

- researching our lineage online

- honoring them through rituals and practices of remembrance (e.g., lighting a candle, placing their photos on an altar, or visiting places significant to family history)

- direct expressions of gratitude for whatever resilience, wisdom, and positive qualities we've inherited from them

- actively listening for messages and themes from past generations

- somatic practices (breathwork, meditation, and so on) to release stored pain and tension

- compassionate witnessing—holding space for their struggles and acknowledging the hardships they endured without judgment

- mindful connection through prayer and intention-setting for any ancestors who actively want to help us heal

> Which of the listed methods of connection have you already practiced? What would you add to the list? With your ancestors in mind, try one out for a week or two and record what comes up for you.

Practice

CONNECTING WITH ANCESTORS

Take a couple of breaths and connect with the sensations in your body. The more attention you pay to your body and the more you drop into this somatic awareness, the more sensations you'll notice. You might also detect a sense of awareness that's paying attention to these sensations.

With attunement to your body, invite any ancestors who might be willing to join you in this healing space. Notice what happens. Notice what comes up when you say, "I invite my close ancestors—my parents, grandparents, and great-grandparents—into this healing space."

Tune into the feeling of who shows up. Notice where there's a sense of flow and connectedness. Which relationships feel most open and supportive? We call these ancestors the "gates." The gates are where you'll find this intergenerational transmission of wisdom, creativity, strength, resilience, intelligence, and the spark of life. Feel this experience in your body. Note any feeling of gratefulness you experience in being a part of such an integrated lineage.

Other ancestors might feel more distant, reduced, or numb. From them, you may notice a diminished flow of information; you might even experience some of their pain. Notice how this shows up in your body too. How do their fear, shame, stress, and so forth live in you?

Bring a witnessing awareness to all of this. Feel all of it. You can even invite some illuminations into the pain parts of those ancestors. The space you've invited them into is a healing space. With them, hold the intention that you may all heal together.

When you feel ready, bring attention back to your body, to your breath. Slowly come back to wherever you're sitting and open your eyes.

Live Session

As you read through this session, feel into how it resonates with you and your process. In this example, how might your ancestors have experienced uprootedness? Witness how this participant begins to integrate some of the intergenerational disconnect. How is that available for you too? As she illustrates, we can all go deeper into an experience that feels painful, even when we feel like we just can't do it.

> **Thomas:** First of all, thank you for your courage and your generosity to go through a process here with me. Do you want to share a little bit about what's important for you and what you want to look at?
>
> **Participant:** Of course. Inner safety has always been an issue for me. I'm a first-generation immigrant from South America, and I came here when I was about twelve years old. My family comes from a lot of displacement, especially my parents. They regularly had to uproot themselves because of war. We come from an Indigenous background, and my father's people are from the mountains, but we don't know what kind of group we belong to. There's no talk about that in our family. There's a lot of history in my family that has been lost.
>
> My mother's side has a lot of sexual assault, so there's a lot of protectiveness that comes from my background,

and in that protectiveness, there's a lot of inner safety issues that I've noticed within myself. I don't feel safe. There's the component of me being a woman as well, but I feel like there's a lot of things that have been passed down within my family and then there's my own experiences where I struggle with inner safety a lot, especially around men. In my own therapy processing with IFS, there's been a lot of work with protective parts around relationships with men. That's what I would love to process today. Just that inner safety part.

Thomas: Let's first look at the safety, and then if we have time, I would love to look at your Indigenous roots. When you talk about the inner safety and you talk about feeling safe or unsafe, how does that live in your body? How do you feel when you feel unsafe, when you're tuning with it now?

Participant: I have anxiety, and it usually transforms into me wanting to hide. I get a lot of physical reactions, especially if I'm in public. Sometimes it feels like I'm trapped in a box and I can't move, so it becomes immobilizing. I used to be more outgoing. I used to be more social, but then my anxiety got worse, especially during the COVID-19 quarantine. Now, I don't go out as much. I feel like I've secluded myself, not just from society, but from friends, just in terms of going out and meeting people. With everything that's been happening in the world, a lot of things come up, and my anxiety kind of kicks in.

Thomas: How does it feel in your body right now? How do you feel?

Participant: I feel it in my chest and my throat and a little bit in my stomach.

Thomas: Okay. Let's focus a little bit of attention on your chest, maybe your throat, and your stomach, and let's gently approach those areas and find out what is there. Maybe there's tension, maybe there's a pressure.

Participant: As I'm observing it, it calms down a little bit. There's more curiosity now because I'm paying attention to it. I don't feel heavy here. My stomach still feels a little unsure.

Thomas: Let's go to the stomach and feel this unsureness and maybe also a bit of stress that's in there.

Participant: It also calmed down now that I'm putting attention to it.

Thomas: Right.

Participant: It wants to talk.

Thomas: Sorry?

Participant: I don't know. It just said, "I want to talk."

Thomas: All right. Is there still that pressure? Did it disappear from throat, chest, belly?

Participant: Yeah.

Thomas: Very good. Emotionally, how do you feel? You said curious?

Participant: Yeah, there's a sense of curiosity. Excitement too, like something is rubbing up inside. I want to laugh.

Thomas: That's good. It's freeing up energy. You said that in public spaces you feel sometimes more boxed in.

Participant: I usually feel like there's a glass around me. It doesn't feel like that now.

Thomas: Now that you feel like your body is a bit more relaxed and open, I want to return to something you said earlier. "My ancestors were often uprooted." When you focus a little bit inside of yourself at the uprootedness of your ancestors, see what body sensations arise and maybe what emotion shows up.

Participant: My hands feel tense. I have this image in my head that hasn't gone away since we started checking in, which is people. It's like a circle. People just kneeling and looking at me, and I feel my hands kind of tensing. I feel it in my chest. Sadness. Anger.

Thomas: Maybe we can give a little bit of space to the emotion you described—sadness and anger—and let the emotion have a bit more space. It can expand a bit in the chest, and it can take more space in you. And see if that's possible then.

Participant: Yeah, it's taking over. The anger mostly.

Thomas: Okay. Let's let the anger take its space and see how it feels when the anger that was compressed can have a bit more space in you.

Participant: It's like I'm hearing it speak. I don't know, it's like words that I don't know what they are, but they want to come out. I feel like screaming. I feel like, I don't know . . .

Thomas: If you let the words that you don't understand, if you let them come out?

Participant: "Home was never ours." That's something that came up. And a lot of "I hate" words. A lot of "not fair." A lot of rejection to others. People who hurt.

Thomas: Let yourself feel what comes with it when you say it.

Participant: A lot of wariness too.

Thomas: Right.

Participant: "We stay away. They hurt us, so we stay away."

Thomas: Check if you have a sense that you've told me these things and I've heard them. Maybe there's no felt connection, maybe there is a little bit. We don't need to change it. We want to just find out how it is.

Participant: Yes. And I think that's why they said they want to speak . . . It's like there's a lot of speak, speak, speak, speak. Just feelings of people running . . . I don't want to say running around, but it's just a lot of words coming at the same time.

Thomas: Pay some attention to the fact that you feel I'm here and that your words and your sense that I'm here happened at the same time. You said, "It was never our home" or "Our home was never ours," and I heard it. I hear that, and it lands in me.

Participant: That feels soothing. The mess went away.

Thomas: And then, when you say it feels soothing, you can also see how that affects your body and your grounding, if that changed the way you feel your body and your grounding or if it stayed the same like before.

Participant: No, I'm very relaxed actually.

Thomas: Let's feel that relaxation, that something could exhale a bit. And some of the inner pressure to speak could relax, as if suddenly words have been heard. Received.

Participant: Yeah.

Thomas: And then, as your body relaxes, maybe you can also feel into the ground and feel the hurt roots of your ancestors. Start examining that. Create your own deeper relationship with the soil by looking at their uprootedness. Check in with how it feels now.

Participant: I usually like walking around barefoot so it gives me comfort when I put my feet on the ground.

Thomas: When you look into your inner space, is there anything more to say from what wanted to speak before, or did this calm down?

Participant: It's calmed down. There's no mess or voices or words trying. Just calm.

Thomas: We looked at some of the uprootedness, and we saw how that needs to integrate itself a bit. Is it okay if we look at the Indigenous cultural heritage? Because I think that could be another step we could do today.

Participant: Mm-hmm.

Thomas: I would love for us to come back to when you said your father's ancestors lived in the mountains, how that feels in you. What comes up when you relate to the echo of that disconnect to your roots and the beauty of their culture?

Participant: I think that's something I've carried always. There's always been a part of me that feels like it's missing. It's something I can't really connect to. Even in terms of my own grandmother. She was apparently the daughter of the leader in the tribe or something. That had been a role in the tribe that had been passed down. But my own father doesn't speak of her. There's not a lot of information on that side. There's a lot of things that have been silenced through history, and we don't even have a connection there.

Thomas: How does that feel? "It has been silenced, and we don't have a connection." Listen. When you listen to your body and see how this silence and the non-connection lives inside, what do you feel when you say that?

Participant: A sense of loneliness comes up. Deep loneliness.

Thomas: Let's feel that loneliness. Loneliness is when we reside somewhere deeper inside. There's a sense of "I'm lonely," but when I'm lonely, I'm also somewhere inside in a cave or in an inner space. Let's see if that resonates when I say this, a kind of inner cave where you sit in yourself and you're a bit lonely when we relate to your Indigenous ancestors. Or, if you have a different experience of loneliness, then describe that.

Participant: It just feels like I'm standing in the darkness. I don't recognize myself. I'm looking at my hands, I'm looking at myself, and it's like there's nothing else around. There's a sense of screaming into the void.

Thomas: I want us to feel a bit into the void. Let's see if some of the cultural disconnect lives in you as a bit of a void or a numbness. Just feel that you don't feel in that place. This darkness is an unfelt space. I feel that I'm not feeling. What happens if you acknowledge that kind of unfelt space?

Participant: It's like pieces of it are falling apart. I definitely see . . . I'm standing in nature, I'm standing with the sun kind of peeking through, but it's not entire . . . It's pieces of it. It's as if it was a wallpaper and it's being ripped off.

Thomas: And then you can feel that something else already shows up. It shows up as sun, as nature, and somehow, there's more information coming to you already, and you can connect to that information and resonate with it.

Participant: I hear . . . it seems like there's children laughing, but I can't see them. It's like laughter I hear. It's like laughter behind whatever nature thing I'm seeing. It feels nice.

Thomas: Let it feel nice. Enjoy that you are coming closer again to a part of you that is stored in your nervous system. That's stored in you because your ancestors live in you, so they are stored in you. And you get access to it and you can enjoy that. I think you also carry something, like what you said about your grandmother, there's something about that strength in you. When I see you, there's something like a kind of a leader quality that you bring. And I think if you enjoy these kind of images that come, they'll connect you to something you carry inside yourself.

Participant: I'm feeling a little teary-eyed right now because it just feels like, for a long time, it's like I've always been trying to find the filling of the void in other people, and the thought that came as I was witnessing and listening to the children . . . it wasn't people; it was something that looks like that. Even hearing the children laughing or something like that was the void, the imagery that came to me. It wasn't people I've been looking for; it was finding my way there.

Thomas: Exactly. I have the feeling that that reconnection that opened, that it could be that the void has been accepted and respected, and it could open up to the next layer in you, and I think that will reconnect you to it. I think it's already happening with some of the strength your ancestors had and some of the beauty, and it fills part of your core and gives you a strength that lives in you. How do you feel now?

Participant: It's like when you're trying to find yourself, there's a sense of always having it within you. You don't search for it outside. I don't think it's ever clicked like it clicked today. Because I thought that what I was looking for inside was a part of me that maybe got disconnected through my own trauma, my own experiences. But going there and connecting with my ancestors and connecting with the history that I don't have a connection with, it just feels like a completely different step, I would say. It feels like it was something I never, never would've thought of doing.

Thomas: It's also touching how it touches you. There's this resonance to your ancestors, how it touches you and how much love there is in you.

Participant: Yeah. It's beautiful. Thank you.

Thomas: Thank you also for sharing the gift with us, especially the part with the void. When we come into these places where we don't feel ourselves and it feels like we're disconnected, we don't know what to do. How you held it in yourself and allowed it to dissipate slowly, I think that's a great learning that it's possible. You got access to something that expands you, and that's also a deep learning for everybody, that we can go through these places and find a deeper treasure in our being there.

Participant: I think I definitely have to keep exploring that side now. There's something there.

Thomas: Definitely. When you sit and meditate a bit on this part, what you felt today, just enjoy it, and it'll come back and speak to you and give you some of that wisdom that's stored in your Indigenous, elder tradition.

Participant: Thank you. I will. Thank you.

The void she describes in this session is a "not feeling," which is a process. You need to do something in order to stop feeling. It requires action. "Not remembering" is an action. Something turned it off in the nervous system, and something can turn it back on again. When we honor not remembering or not feeling as important functions, they can slowly change into something else. We don't force memories to come back. We don't have to. Some of the things we experienced or did in the past clearly aren't needed or useful anymore, but they were at one time. We have to honor that too. Focusing on the absence, the void, brought this participant's ancestors forward, and they weren't solely focused on their burdens. They offered their gifts as well.

> Is there anything you're aware of not feeling? Or not remembering? When it comes to your ancestors, what's your experience of encountering a void?

Practice

ANCESTORS AND LEGACY BURDENS

Take a few moments to focus inside. While reading the previous session, something may have come up for you. Maybe it's compassion for someone you received a legacy burden from, or maybe it's more awareness of how you inherited something powerful from one of your ancestors.

Pay attention to whatever emotion or belief comes up. Find it in your body. As you're paying attention in this way, see if any ancestors show up. Sometimes there's more than one, and in those cases, it can be a good idea to ask them to take turns speaking because once you open the door, they can rush the gate, so to speak. And if they don't come, just invite them to enter the space now. Simply invite any ancestors who might be related to these emotions, sensations, or beliefs to come in, and see who shows up.

Often, when we do this practice, it's a good idea to ask the rational parts of us to relax for a little while. If they hang around too much, commenting and analyzing everything, it's unlikely anything will happen.

Focus on whatever ancestors show up. Ask them if there's anything they want you to know about this legacy burden you carry inside of you. Ask them about the source of it. Do they want you to continue to carry it, or not? Would they also like to unload it? Do they believe they need to keep carrying it? Think of any questions you'd like to clarify and ask them.

They may or may not be ready to give up the legacy burden. If they do want to unload it, ask them how they think that should happen. There are all sorts of ways to send a burden out of your system. Some involve offering it to the elements—earth, light, water, fire, and so on.

Sometimes ancestors might not want to send the burden too far away. Maybe they want to keep an eye on it. In these cases, you could place the burden in a special box. That way, you both don't have to carry it, but you also won't forget about it.

If you get any clarity about what to do, do it. Let the legacy burden out of you, out of them, whatever feels most appropriate and wanted. If you can do this practice, you might feel a palpable shift in your body. If you can't, that's okay too. Sometimes it takes a lot more exploration to begin this level of healing.

Whatever happens, thank the ancestors for coming and speaking with you. Then start to shift your focus back outside again, back into the present reality.

Other Considerations

Connecting to our ancestors—especially those from multiple generations back—can prove difficult when there's something in our lineage blocking access. Those of us with colonizers in our ancestry may meet additional obstacles, as human rights violations and ethical transgressions typically interfere with this information stream. If you reach back and it feels like it's not working, it could be that you're trying to move through spaces that need to be surfaced first. Before contacting those ancestors, you will likely first have to address their shame and guilt. Doing so will foster deeper relations all the way down the line.

When transgressions are part of the lineage, it can be hard to relate with them. We might instinctively turn away, reject that part of our lineage, or hold strong judgments as a shield against feeling the pain. When we bring curiosity and inquire about our reaction, we can soften and open up more. From that place, we can ask our ancestors how they feel about what happened. In doing so, we build a bridge step by step. This process can awaken a deeper felt sense and allow for restoration, intergenerational learning, and a maturation of the ancestral line.

Of course, some of us know very little about our ancestors. If you were adopted, for example, the split between you and your lineage can feel insurmountable. When you don't have the information you need to begin this work, trying to access your ancestors can feel like running into a wall of impenetrable numbness. We usually can't penetrate these kinds of obstacles by ourselves, which is why it can be helpful to work with a professional. In the case of working with the generational trauma associated with adoption, a safe space is crucial. Trying harder by yourself doesn't usually help. But you can always tune into your body in the places where you *are* integrated, where you *do* have access to sensations, and expand from there. It can also help to focus on the subtler ways that ancestral influences show up (in our intuition and dreams, for example).

6

Trauma and Spirituality

Defining Spirituality

Spirituality is the living, embodied experience of interconnectedness and presence rather than a set of beliefs or doctrines. It is often correlated with profound mystical states that some think of as oneness, union with the Divine, enlightenment, nonduality, and so on. Different traditions explain these experiences in various ways, and many would assert that there are several steps or levels to spiritual awakening. Whatever one calls these states, they're broadly associated with the dissolution of one's normal sense of identity while directly accessing an inexplicable sense of something larger, deeper, more encompassing, more fluid, and far more expansive than our daily personalities and sense of reality could ever express or fathom.

To be clear, when we talk about spirituality, we're not simply referring to mystical experiences and the practices one might take to access them. In our understanding, spirituality isn't separate from daily life. Our spirituality calls us to expand our awareness of both inner and outer realities, creating a sense of harmony or unity with ourselves, others, and the larger fabric of life. Sometimes that means tapping into a timeless space in which we feel connected to a greater essence beyond the limitations of the mind, but spirituality is also expressed in less esoteric ways—how we speak to ourselves, how we care for others, and how well we love the world. In this way, spirituality is essentially the understanding that we're all part of a greater, interdependent reality. Our spiritual practices, therefore, inspire us to increase our inner awareness to more fully participate in all of the sacred activities of life.

An Inexhaustible Resource

Thankfully, spirituality is an endless resource. It's not like monetary wealth or any other kind of worldly privilege. Spirituality is accessible to everyone. Becoming more aware that we're interconnected with the big picture—whether we call it God, the Tao, Ātman, Buddha-nature, the Great Mystery, the Big Self, or some other name—allows us more access to our Self and our Self-energy. In the process, we don't transcend our daily lives or evolve into partless beings who don't experience the challenges that come with being human. Spirituality isn't an out; it's the ultimate resource.

> What does spirituality mean to you? How has your spirituality been a resource to you over the years? What's lacking in your spiritual life?

Spirituality supports us as individuals and communities to navigate challenges, heal trauma, and foster greater connection and understanding. It's a source of inner strength, resilience, and wisdom that can guide us through difficult experiences and empower us to engage with the complexities of life in a more integrated and conscious way. Spirituality is also a fount of creativity and inspiration that allows us to access intuitive insights and creative impulses that arise from beyond the ordinary mind.

Spiritual principles like compassion, non-judgment, and empathy offer a foundation for making decisions and acting in ways that are aligned with a sense of deeper truth. Spirituality can nurture a sense of connection and purpose. It supports us to foster presence, access insights, and participate in the larger unfolding of life. Through spirituality, we can find the resilience, clarity, and compassion needed to live more fully and contribute positively to the world around us.

Our spirituality enriches the world. It's not about acquiring some blissful, light-filled, personal experience of the Divine. Our spirituality has agency here in this world. The world is enhanced by our spiritual practices, and when we free up stuck information with our spirituality, we increase the possibilities in a world that too often lacks them. The planet and the people who inhabit it are not a finite set of beings in a stuck system. The system is interdependent with us, and so our lives—including our spirituality—are forever changing in constant exchange with it.

DICK'S SPIRITUAL JOURNEY

I come from an atheistic, scientific family. My father was a prominent physician/researcher, and three of my five brothers are physicians. As the eldest, I was expected to become a physician too. I was spared that fate (I didn't excel in school because of my undiagnosed ADD), but that left me with a heavy dose of worthlessness. I also shared my family's skepticism for all things spiritual.

I graduated college with no clear direction and lots of anxiety and then ran into Transcendental Meditation® (TM).

While I wasn't interested in the spirituality of TM, I did find that it could help with my insecurity and anxiety. With my mantra, I could access a wonderfully calm, clear, and confident state that helped me navigate those challenging years of the seventies and keep away that gnawing sense of worthlessness.

In retrospect, I see that while practicing TM did help me a lot at that time, I was also using it to bypass, rather than heal, my exiles. It also piqued my curiosity about why it worked and, thus, opened a crack in my protective fortress around spirituality. Then, in the eighties, clients began speaking of their parts, I began developing IFS, and because I was so busy, I stopped meditating. As I helped clients identify and separate from their parts, often they would suddenly and spontaneously access a state of calmness, confidence, and clarity relative to their parts, which reminded me of the state I had accessed through TM. I came to call that the Self, but I still had a materialistic view of what it was: a part of the personality, albeit very helpful and, unlike other parts I was encountering, neither extreme nor burdened. That was hard to reconcile with the horrible childhoods my clients had described to me.

Over time, that issue became harder and harder to reconcile and some students kept pushing the idea that what we were encountering was akin to Buddha-nature, Christ Consciousness, or Nephesh. As I explored that terrain (see *Many Minds, One Self*, the book I coauthored with Bob Falconer), I became less skeptical and more excited by the possibility that Self could be a spiritual essence. Now, over forty years later, I'm quite convinced that the Self in each of us is a drop of a bigger ocean that has various names, including the nondual, God, or the Big Self. Just as a photon is both particle and wave, Self is the particle state of a much larger wave. This is the best explanation for why it can't be damaged and why it inherently knows how to heal. It also explains why we feel so much more connected to one another when we access Self—at the wave-state level, we're all connected.

I still consider myself a scientist, and the most influential piece of advice my father ever gave me was to follow the data, even if it takes you way outside your paradigm. Following the trail of IFS took me way outside the traditional standard, and if I'm proud of anything, it's that I followed it, despite the constant drone of my skeptical parts. I now consider myself to be quite spiritual and am thrilled to be able to continue exploring the nonmaterial world this way.

THOMAS'S SPIRITUAL JOURNEY

Growing up, I felt very much connected to God, but not necessarily to the Catholic Church in the village of my childhood. I started meditating daily when I was nineteen, and the practice stuck with me as I went through my medical studies. I worked as a volunteer paramedic for the Red Cross for several years, but at some point, I felt a strong calling to do something different with my life, although I wasn't sure what it was. I just knew I had to find a way to open up and explore my inner world somehow, and the calling to do so became stronger and stronger. So much so that I decided to leave school in my mid-twenties and immerse myself in a four-year, self-guided meditation retreat.

When I look back on those years, I marvel at how much guidance I received, especially during the retreat. Four years of meditating wasn't exactly easy, but it was necessary for me to live and serve in the ways I do today. You can imagine that my family wasn't very happy about my decision to abandon my medical studies, but I convinced them that I was still studying, just in a new way. Later, I also went back to school to finish my PhD, focusing on trauma and healing. I couldn't have done that without choosing a different path and immersing myself in the spiritual path that called to me.

Over time, I understood that even though, in a sense, I left the world to go on retreat, spirituality isn't about leaving life behind or finding a way to get away from daily struggles. Spirituality is about deepening *into* life and becoming more present with everything the world has to offer. When we approach our spirituality in this way, it becomes an incredible resource for healing and transformation.

Spirituality and the Collective

Spiritual experiences are not only personal, but they are also intricately tied to the collective field of humanity. Spirituality isn't just about individual enlightenment or awakening; it's about how our inner experiences connect with, contribute to, and are influenced by the larger collective. Geometrically, we can think of spiritual practice on the vertical axis, whereas collective work is more of the horizontal expansion of our relational capacity. Spirituality is also the emergence or innovation that flows through the higher consciousness to all the people who are receptive to it. Many call that process *creativity*. Participating in the creative impulse of the universe upgrades and evolves the collective.

The collective field can both limit and enhance our spiritual journey, depending on how we engage with it. Collective beliefs can limit our spiritual growth if they reinforce narrow views or restrictive dogmas. Inherited wounds can create inner barriers that prevent individuals from accessing deeper states of presence or spiritual insight. Working through collective trauma is a critical part of deepening one's spirituality, as it allows us to reclaim parts of ourselves that have been fragmented or shut down. And unless we tap into the spiritual resourcing inherent in collective trauma processes, we will remain caught up in our cultural space. On the other hand, cultures can also nurture spiritual development through their respective rich traditions, rituals, and practices that foster a sense of connection, meaning, and transcendence.

We are constantly immersed in collective energy fields, which affect our consciousness and spiritual states. The energy of a group can create a supportive environment in which individuals can more easily access deeper states of presence, insight, and healing. For example, as we explored earlier, when people come together with a shared intention for meditation or healing, they create a resonant field that can amplify spiritual experiences. On the other hand, when immersed in a collective environment filled with fear, anger, or division, individuals may find it more challenging to maintain their spiritual clarity and openness. Being aware of the collective energy field and learning to navigate it consciously can help individuals maintain a connection to their own spiritual center while being part of a larger community.

During group retreats, there's usually a point at which people feel a greater sense of connectedness with each other. Sometimes we think of this as the collective Self. Whatever you call it, there's an enhanced sense of safety. People become more vulnerable and a sense of trust begins to snowball, making each person's work that much deeper.

THOMAS

Often, when I work with both Jewish participants and descendants of the German Schutzstaffel/Nazi regime together (and sometimes with descendants of Holocaust survivors in the same room), amongst other collective trauma fields, I experience the emergence of a much deeper collective presence. When that happens, you can hear a pin drop in the room. Everyone is plugged into something much bigger, as if a collective witness has emerged. As the sensitivity of the topic opens up, there may be different opinions in the room or activated responses, which is normal. However, there are moments when we emerge into a higher state as a collective. In groups, sometimes we can achieve a level of healing or breakthrough in minutes that might otherwise take multiple sessions. The energy is just so high in the room that everything becomes more fluid and open. The more we elevate our consciousness, the processes and data flow much faster and the intelligence frees up, which means that healing happens faster too.

Practice

YOUR INNER SCREENSHOT—THOMAS

Start by taking a breath, feeling your body, and taking an inner screenshot. How do you feel right now? Notice your physical, emotional, mental, and relational states, given everything that's happening in your life. Just notice. Don't try to change anything. Just notice if you're stressed, if you're relaxed, if you're agitated emotionally, calm, mentally busy, or relaxed. Just notice.

Focus a bit more on your breath, specifically your exhalations. Every time you exhale, let the breath connect you to your body sensations and notice where your body is most vibrant, energized, flowing, streaming, pulsing, and present.

Also notice how feeling your body is a way to connect to the ground underneath you. If you're more relaxed, it's easier to connect to the ground. If you're more stressed, your energy pushes upward. Just notice how it is. Don't force it. Just notice.

Exhale your experience. Digest it. When you digest, you're grounding yourself to integrate your experience as learning. As you feel your body sensations and your grounding, you can also notice that which is aware of how you feel. Feel your body. Become aware that you feel your body and notice that awareness. Don't ponder what's aware. Just notice the awareness.

In that deeper witnessing space, connect to what Dick calls Self or Self-energy, or what I think of as the essence of the soul that meets the integrated Self. Whatever you call the spiritual dimension of your life, bring it into this session so it can reveal itself more and bring insights, understanding, revelations, and inner teaching.

To conclude, slowly bring your attention back into your heart and extend your awareness to the larger community of practitioners. You might not know who they are or when they're doing this exercise, but know that there are other people all around the world interested in healing and contributing to the healing of our world. Take a moment to pay attention to this collective, then slowly open your eyes and come back.

Trauma and Spirituality

Trauma and its subsequent burdens can make it more difficult for us to access our spirituality and enjoy transformational spiritual experiences, hindering the expression of our Self-energy. Trauma often acts as a barrier to spiritual growth, creating disconnection and polarization in our inner world. When people are caught in the unresolved memories or patterns of trauma, they often find it difficult to access deeper states of meditative awareness or spiritual presence. But these very spiritual practices are what can help soothe the more fearful parts of ourselves and give us more of a chance to access our true Self. There are dimensions or realms that are normally hidden to us that contain entities and energies that want to help us and actively do so when they can. Unburdening facilitates that assistance.

Understanding and integrating trauma is essential for authentic spiritual growth, and it can serve as a gateway to transformative experiences and enhanced spiritual awareness. We must work through the energetic blocks of trauma to become more present and aware of the deeper dimensions of life. Facing and integrating our wounds creates opportunities to expand our consciousness and further our understanding of ourselves and others. By working through trauma, we can access new levels of compassion, empathy, and wisdom. This process allows us to transform pain into insight, making the journey of healing a profound spiritual practice. Addressing collective trauma in particular is a spiritual responsibility, as it allows individuals to contribute to the healing of the collective field and expand our awareness beyond ourselves. Healing from trauma enables deeper states of presence, expanding our capacity for connection and allowing for a more integrated and authentic spiritual experience that goes far beyond our individual benefit.

Healing from Spiritual Trauma

Spiritual trauma is a profound wound that occurs when our fundamental trust in life, existence, or spiritual dimensions is broken or distorted. This kind of trauma can occur through personal experiences, such as abuse in a spiritual context, or through collective experiences, such as societal or religious oppression. Spiritual trauma can have deep and long-lasting effects on how individuals relate to themselves, others, and their sense of the Divine.

When this trust is broken, individuals may feel disconnected from their inner guidance, struggle with feelings of abandonment or isolation, and lose their sense of purpose or meaning in life. Spiritual trauma can also result in an inability to trust one's own spiritual experiences or an enduring fear of encountering the unknown aspects of consciousness. When spiritual ideas are weaponized against a person's sense of worth or humanity, it can create a damaging sense of unworthiness or fear of divine judgment. This type of trauma can lead individuals to feel that they are fundamentally flawed or that they must conform to rigid spiritual standards to be worthy of love and connection.

When spiritual teachings or experiences push individuals to deny or reject parts of themselves (such as emotions or desires) or deem them as being "unspiritual" or "impure," it can create a kind of inner fragmentation in which certain aspects of the Self are cut off in an attempt to conform to spiritual ideals. This leaves individuals feeling ungrounded, disconnected from their bodies, and unable to access the wholeness of their being. When spiritual trauma results from experiences in spiritual communities or under the guidance of spiritual leaders, it can lead to a profound mistrust of spiritual teachings, leaders, and communities.

To heal from spiritual trauma, one must cultivate presence as a way to restore trust in oneself and life. Through practices like meditation, mindfulness, and self-inquiry, individuals can learn to reconnect with their inner essence beyond the layers of trauma. Healing often involves integrating the fragmented parts of oneself that have been disconnected or suppressed with an attitude of compassionate curiosity, in which we gently explore the parts of ourselves that may have been rejected in the name of spirituality.

Ultimately, a person who has suffered from spiritual trauma can reclaim their relationship with spirituality without mediation from external authorities or rigid doctrines. This involves discovering a personal sense of the sacred, which can be more expansive, open, and rooted in direct experience. There is also tremendous healing power when engaging with conscious, supportive groups that help individuals process their wounds to find a new sense of belonging.

SPIRITUAL STRUGGLE, SPIRITUAL GUIDES—DICK

Over time, I've come across what some people refer to as "guides." When I encounter them in my IFS sessions, they usually assert they're not a part of the client but are external entities. As I've come to know my guides better, they've made it clear that I'm simply channeling their wisdom, that all my work isn't just the product of my individual little brain. What a relief! After I heard that, I relaxed a lot and was less attached to the IFS model. IFS is designed to open more space for that kind of wisdom to enter—wisdom from guides, wisdom from God—all of which is crucially important in the world today. Our parts and their burdens might make connecting to our guides more challenging, but as we do the work of unburdening, our parts return to their naturally valuable states. In turn, the beneficial energies have much more access to us.

Live Session

This last session is with a close friend of mine who was an AIDS advocate, IFS master therapist, and loving father. I did a longer session with him as he was nearing the end of his life, and am including a lightly edited version of it here, as it highlights his spiritual journey, his relationship with his guides, and his ongoing relationship with his parts after receiving his terminal cancer diagnosis.

> **Client:** It's a little bit surreal. I'm feeling okay, man. The side of my tongue has gone numb, which is really annoying because it makes it hard to teach because I'm speaking strange, but at the same time, I'm talking to the palliative care doctor. In Canada, we have medical assistance in dying, so I've got a doctor coming on Tuesday to sign off on that, so when I'm ready to go, she can just come and give me the injection. And I just got back from Mexico with my daughter, so it's a bit strange.
>
> **Dick:** And what's the prognosis?
>
> **Client:** It was diagnosed as metastasized in July, so it's gone to the lungs as well as the throat. I think what's likely to happen is the tumor here is just going to keep growing unchecked. At some point, it's going to press against the esophagus or the larynx or burst some blood vessels, and at that point, it'll probably become unendurable. So that's what I have to make a decision about. It could be two months, could be four, could be less . . .
>
> **Dick:** How do you feel about it? I heard you say "surreal."

Client: It seems like each progressive shift brings up parts that are grieving, parts that don't want to go, parts that don't want to leave my daughter. She's only twenty. And at the same time, I've got this main narrative in my system that I'm being called home. That's my understanding. And that my body's response to being called home is to generate the cancer because it's the only way it can facilitate those steps home, which is part of the mystery. But to me, that provides a lot of comfort. At least there's some way of making meaning from this, which feels genuine.

Dick: And the narrative came from guidance?

Client: No, I was doing some medicine work with a shaman, and I received or downloaded that information that's what the cancer is.

Dick: That's what I mean by guidance.

Client: Yeah. Oh yeah, guidance.

Dick: But it's still probably hard for all of your parts to believe.

Client: Most of them are on board. Actually, at the moment as I'm talking to you, it feels like they're all on board. I might be missing a couple, but what I'm hearing is that some of them still don't want to go. What I've been guided to is the process of transitioning to becoming an ancestor, and that's what this transition of consciousness is about. But even then I can hear, "Yeah, but I don't want to transition to becoming a fucking ancestor!" I also have a manager that's using that as an attempt to spiritually bypass because every time one of these parts comes up with protest; it says, "No, no, we're transitioning to becoming an ancestor." I have to keep that one in check. Otherwise it'll be the only allowable narrative, and these other parts just need to be witnessed, I think.

Dick: Totally makes sense. So, did you have thoughts about how to use this time?

Client: Yeah. I wanted to see what's up for me and if I'm missing something. And I thought you'd be the guy to help me do that because you know me so well . . . I'm also having a surge of love for you, and maybe this will be the last time I see you, so . . .

Dick: I love you too, man.

Client: The goodbyes are the hardest.

Dick: I bet. Yeah. So we can just go in and see if you're missing anything. We could also try to get more access to your guides. And we could also see if there's anything the cancer wants you to know. All of those are possible.

Client: It doesn't feel like I'm missing anything. It feels like I've been quite clean in that process. The guides . . . usually I have access to them when I'm working with medicine. I realize I could probably have access without the medicine. The last time I attempted to encounter the cancer as an entity, it was confused. It was confused about what was going on. However, at the time, I had an agenda to try and get rid of it, basically. So I wasn't coming with a ton of Self-energy. We can maybe go that route.

Dick: That sounds good. We'll just see. There might be parts that have been using the cancer and have a message for you. Are you ready?

Client: I just had a reaction when you said that. There's a part saying, "Hang on . . . does that mean we brought the cancer on ourselves and we want to die? Is that what Dick's saying?"

Dick: No, not a bit.

Client: All right. That part panicked.

Dick: See if it'll give us some space. So go ahead and focus on the cancer again and see where you find it mostly in your body or around your body.

Client: Well, I know it's in the throat and the lungs, but it feels like it's here [rubs the right side of his neck]. This is the main one. This is the one that is growing rapidly.

Dick: Okay, how do you feel toward it?

Client: The word "companion" comes up. *Companionable.*

Dick: Okay, good. Let it know you feel that way toward it.

Client: I'm getting a visual of us walking together.

Dick: See if there is something that it wants you to know or the parts that are involved want you to know.

Client: It feels very peaceful. I'm reminded of a Ram Dass expression: "We're just walking each other home." It's surprising. There's not a lot of energy there, just a sense of walking *with*. Like we're both people. Two people.

Dick: Ask it about itself. If there's something about it that it wants you to know.

Client: Well, I can't tell if I'm making up a reply or if there's a part of me doing that or if I'm hearing from it. Can you help me with that?

Dick: We'll see. See what the response is.

Client: All right. So what I'm experiencing is it's linking arms with me and it's kind of just like, "Yeah, it's how it is."

Dick: Maybe ask if it's come to do that, to take you home.

Client: It's nodding, yeah.

Dick: Okay. Anything it wants you to know about this particular time and why it came now?

Client: It's got regret about bringing pain, which I appreciate. It's time.

Dick: Maybe ask if it made that decision or was it sent?

Client: Very clear. It was sent.

Dick: Can it reveal who sent it?

Client: Yeah. I just . . . I'm getting information very rapidly. So what it's showing me is this . . . immense . . . I think it's attempting to show me God.

Dick: Stay with that. Tell it you're ready to see God.

Client: I'm feeling very tiny. I felt this immense surge of love for me. Not just now, but through all the ages of me this time around, this incarnation.

Dick: That's right. That's fantastic. Just stay with all that.

Client: I'm back to feeling peaceful. I'm back to feeling very much my age. Very present.

Dick: You still have the connection to God?

Client: It feels like it's there, but . . . it's not that dramatic. It's simply a presence. A connection.

Dick: How does it feel to know that's who sent this cancer?

Client: It's good. It's confirming what I experienced in the medicine work. There are parts of me that can dismiss medicine work and invalidate it, so it feels very good to get that affirmation outside of that context.

Dick: That's great. Maybe just see if God or the cancer . . . if there's anything else it wants you to know.

Client: What I'm hearing from God is *Beloved child.*

Dick: Say it again.

Client: *Beloved child* . . .

Dick: How does it feel? Just stay with the awareness of how much God loves you.

Client: So comforting.

Dick: Bring in all the parts that are skeptical about this or afraid to leave so they can bathe in this love too.

Client: Thank you. What I'm hearing now is *Beloved children.* There's one that's frightened, one that doesn't understand . . .

Dick: But can they feel the love?

Client: I'm inviting them to step forward. It's coming to them a bit like light, but more like this really strong, loving presence. It's calming them.

Dick: That's great.

Client: You know how kids, like five-year-olds, will put their face up to the sun? That's what they're doing. They're smiling.

Dick: Let them all know this is where you're going.

Client: I'm also letting them know that we're going to pain-manage the journey as much as we can. What they're scared of is the pain, or some of them are. I'm letting them know it won't get too bad. I'm not . . . I'm not gonna . . .

Dick: Yeah, there's no reason to stay.

Client: We're going to go when we're all ready.

Dick: That's right. And is your daughter going to be around?

Client: It's funny you should ask. We've been able to have some very good conversations. Yes, she'll be around. But I also told her that she'll need to let me go or I will not be able to go, so she has some work to do there. But I've got her hooked up with an IFS therapist, so that should help.

Dick: It might also help her to watch this video.

Client: Good idea. Thank you.

Dick: So let's just check on those parts now, see how everybody's doing.

Client: I'm holding them in my arm, and there's a cluster of them in a meadow, and the sun is shining on them, and the love is shining on them and bathing them, and every one of them has turned their faces up to that experience, and they're just . . . they're all calm.

Dick: That's great.

Client: Normally, there's at least one polarity in my system, but this isn't.

Dick: This is the way you're going to want to go. Everybody together, everybody ready.

Client: The funny one just said, "We're not ready yet!"

Dick: Go to that one and just see what it needs.

Client: It's showing me a Monty Python scene where they bring the dead cart around and somebody's not ready to go. But beneath the humor, it's also saying, "Just make sure you check in with us all."

Dick: What do you say?

Client: There's a part of me that's made decisions around suffering already. And that decision is I will not have a tracheotomy. But I'm aware now that that's a part that's made that decision, and if it comes to a recommendation of a tracheotomy and a part of me decides "No, that's it, we're done" . . . That's what this one's concerned about. So I'm letting him know that I will revisit if that becomes an option, and we'll see who's up and who's ready because to some parts, that feels unendurable—to live with a tracheotomy—but other parts are saying, "We might not be ready then." So that's a good clarity to have.

Dick: Everybody should be on board and have a voice. Let them know you're going to make sure that's the case.

Client: Okay. Now I've got the polarity! One of them has turned around, two of them have turned around, and said, "We're not having a fucking tracheotomy!"

Dick: Okay. All right. Well, let's bring both sides together and you kind of mediate for them.

Client: The part of them that don't want the tracheotomy are showing me a hole in my throat and various videos that we've seen . . . just ghastly. They don't want that. And then these other parts don't want to die frightened. And then the ones that don't want the tracheotomy have agreed that they will if that becomes necessary. They'll revisit that. They're willing to if their choice means that these other ones are so frightened when we pass. They're willing to renegotiate that.

Dick: That's great.

Client: They're very kind. I mean, they just have their own fear. They don't want to live with the tracheotomy.

Dick: Maybe ask a little more about that fear.

Client: It's the loss. I won't be able to talk. I won't be able to teach. I won't be able to sing. So much that gives my life meaning and purpose . . .

Dick: That makes sense. How's that for the other parts?

Client: They're nodding. They're hugging each other, and they're saying this isn't easy for any of them. The others are still basking in that, the presence of love. It's like these others . . . four of them, like two sets of brothers. They're just agreeing that this is not easy. It's not easy. But I can feel their respect for each other. They're not polarized anymore. They're respectful.

Dick: Remind them that you'll be there the whole time, as will God.

Client: That's so sweet. They're like, "Oh, yeah!" When they get going like this with each other, they completely forget about me and God, and it's all about this [bumps fists together]. So it's very sweet to have them go, "Oh, yeah!" and comforting for them too.

Dick: See if either side carries any burdens they want to unload.

Client: Fear of dying. I've got family stories the parts reminded me of. I'm not sure if these are landing on these parts or not, but one family story is actually one thing I remember. It's when I almost drowned in a swimming pool when I was seven. But a family story that may connect, I don't know yet, is being extremely asthmatic as a baby and going blue, being unable to breathe. I was rushed to the hospital for adrenaline injections. But that's a remembering part, so I don't know if that's accurately coming from these.

Dick: Just ask the parts directly if they carry any of that or anything else that doesn't belong to them. My understanding is once you die, a lot of it gets unloaded or maybe all of it.

Client: That's my understanding too. Yeah, so the ones that are frightened of dying are saying—it's very much in kid language—they're saying, "What if we stop? What if we just stop?" That's their fear. That they're not going to continue.

Dick: What do you mean?

Client: That death is the end of everything for them.

Dick: Oh. Well, tell them that's not true. I mean, you could ask God.

Client: Okay, so they're saying, "How do you know?" so I'm showing them some of the guidance I've received, which somehow they weren't included in, but they can see it now. I'm showing them this dancing state of bliss, eternal infinite bliss. That's good. One of them says, "Wow!"

Dick: That's great.

Client: He's smiling, and he doesn't have the fear of death now. And his buddy—the one next to him is like a kid brother—he's like, "Oh, yeah!"

Dick: That's fantastic. Just check around and see if there's anybody who's still afraid.

Client: No.

Dick: Great. So it's feeling pretty good in there.

Client: Yeah.

Dick: Good. I can't remember what else . . . Does that take care of it all?

Client: You gave three options. We could come to the cancer, hear from the guides, which we have. Is your experience of God and the guides that they're synonymous?

Dick: Well, sort of. In the sense that they're sent by God and they're part of God, but then they are also separate. Sort of like we're drops of that big ocean too—the Self and the body—but we're also part of it, so it's the same idea.

Client: Well, they all feel very settled.

Dick: You could ask if there's anything they want you to do. Or are there any people you want to connect with to feel complete?

Client: No. I told you I'm writing a book about this process, so they're telling me to do that. I don't type, so I'm making as many videos as I can ahead of time. I want to make a set of videos for my daughter for every birthday that I'm not here, and I may need to make videos to the people that will be here when I pass because if I can't talk, I want them to be able to hear about the gifts they've given me. That's the only thing the parts are saying. You know, "Get on that." Because I already can't talk properly, and they don't know how fast . . . like if my tongue becomes completely numb, it's going to be useless. I won't be able to talk, so that's the only thing they're concerned about. Like, "Make sure you do that soon."

Dick: If you want, you can ask the cancer if it's in a big hurry or not, whether it could slow things down a little . . .

Client: A part of me—it must be an English part—that says, *"That's rude, you can't just ask to slow things down."*

Dick: It can always say no.

Client: All right, let me see. Actually, the question I want to ask is, "Can you let me speak? Can you let me continue to speak?" You know what . . . there's a part of me that's so scared to hear no that it's not allowing me to ask.

Dick: Okay, let's work with that part. What's its fear? If you heard no?

Client: I won't be able to talk and I won't be able to say the things I so dearly want to say to the people I love. I won't have time.

Dick: Well, my experience with these cancer things is they can negotiate some, usually.

Client: All right. Great. Let's give it a shot. Thanks. That was really good for that one to hear. Okay, oh . . . a real quick response. I felt an easing back, a pulling back. So that feels like a yes.

Dick: Let him know you appreciate that.

Client: So much. Oh, thank you.

Dick: And make sure it knows you're not trying to get out of going. You just want to make sure it's complete before you go.

Client: Yeah, it knows. It's giving me the thumbs up. All right. Yeah. My sense is that somehow it can maintain the cancer, can maintain its agenda without taking my voice so soon. There are other ways it can operate, which is good because my skeptical part said, "Well, we'll have to wait and see, won't we?"

Dick: Check with that part and see about its fear of believing, its fear of being disappointed.

Client: "Don't put all your eggs in one basket." Follow up with whatever doctors I need to see about the tongue being numb and if there are treatments for it that kind of thing.

Dick: Yeah, I suspect the cancer is okay with that too. But ask the skeptic to not erase the possibility, you know what I'm saying?

Client: Yeah, he's not interested in doing that, but he wants to make sure he's showed me this image of me going with blind faith. That's good. "Check with the doctors." Okay, that's all it's concerned about.

Dick: That works. Anything else we can do at this point?

Client: I think this session is going to become a touchstone for me, so I'm going to return to it if I get kind of wobbly. It's been a lovely experience, and it'll be a lovely reminder. It's one of the reasons I'm so grateful to you. At this point in my life, I've been able to do so much work with the parts around this that I haven't gotten stuck in fear, and I haven't gotten stuck back in despair, and I've been able to attend to them. And that would not have been possible had I never met you. So much to be thankful for.

Dick: You're very welcome. I'm going to miss you.

Client: Part of me says, "I'll see you soon."

Dick: Soon enough. Soon enough.

> What experiences can you relate to in the client's live session? If you can resonate with the concept of spiritual guides or God, what's that like for you? What current challenges in your life might your guides (or spirituality in general) be able to help you with?

Practice

APPROACHING YOUR GUIDES—DICK

If you're interested in trying something IFS-related about spirituality, take a second and focus inside. If you've followed along in the book or have done some IFS work before, you're probably somewhat familiar with your parts now. I'm going to invite you to ask all your parts to come online now and join you at the base of a path.

This could be an actual path somewhere in the world you're familiar with, or it could be something you're visualizing for the first time. Just help your parts assemble there at the base. Help them get comfortable, then ask them to wait there at the base for a few minutes so you can go on a journey without them.

There might be parts that are afraid to let that happen, and that's okay. If they're too afraid, don't even try to go. You can just work with their fears, much like we've done in other exercises. It might also help to have parts that aren't afraid take care of those who are so you can go on this short journey. If you do get permission to go, head out on the path at whatever pace feels right.

As you begin, notice if you're watching yourself walk on that path as if you were outside your body (like seeing yourself as a character in a movie). When that happens, it's usually a manager part who's running the visualization. That's fairly common, so if that's your experience, ask that part to return to the base of the path with the other parts so you can go on the journey without watching yourself at the same time. See if that's possible and, if so, continue along the path.

As you continue, you may notice some thoughts and emotions traveling along with you. For example, you might feel worried about how you're doing or if you're doing the practice right. Those concerns or nagging thoughts are parts too, and you can ask them to return to the base so you can keep going on the journey with more and more attention paid to the journey itself. You might have to repeat this step several times. That's okay. Ideally, as you progress along the path, your awareness will become more prominent than your thoughts and emotions.

If this happens for you, you might notice a kind of vibrating warm energy entering your body, particularly making your fingers and toes tingle. That's a sure sign of Self-energy. Feeling those sensations, ask if there are any guides present who'd like to speak, or any other energy that might want to offer guidance. As before, let the response come to you. There's no effort required at all. It could be that nothing comes up, but also be sure to not rule out something that doesn't fit what you expect. Guidance often arrives in unexpected ways.

When the time feels right, take the path back to the base at whatever pace feels right. As you approach the collection of parts there awaiting your return, they may want to jump back in right away and resume what they usually do. Instead, ask them to wait a little bit so you can be with them in this non-thinking place, with all this vibrating energy, before they become you again, and just see how they react to seeing you this way.

If they let you go on this journey (and it's fine if they didn't), thank them for taking that risk of staying separate from you for a few minutes, and let them know if they allow this every so often, it'll be better for you and them. Finally, ask the parts back in and shift your focus back outside again whenever it feels right. Taking deep breaths at this point often helps.

Ego, Trauma, and Spiritual Bypassing

Some spiritual traditions encourage the eradication of the ego. This is unfortunate because what's typically referred to as the "ego" is simply a collection of little manager parts that are doing their best to keep us safe. It's not helpful to vilify them or treat them as annoying impediments to the spiritual path, which can often backfire, cause us more pain, or reignite our traumas.

It's true that parts sometimes cause us trouble, but it's far better to approach them with curiosity and compassion rather than trying to shoo them away or get rid of them. If you do that, they will gradually come to trust Self and allow it to take leadership of your life. Ideally, the spiritual path isn't about transcending your parts; it's about helping them unburden and transform so they can come along with you on the path.

PSYCHEDELICS AND OTHER MEDICINES

When taken with intention, certain medicines can facilitate nourishing spiritual experiences. Parts of us that are normally managing our experience and access to deeper states suddenly relax or go offline, so to speak, and the healing we can attain as a result can happen a lot more expediently. Some might refer to these experiences as "egoless," when in truth it's just that your manager parts have temporarily allowed something else to arise. We don't consider the medicine itself to be the healing agent; the medicine is

> simply a tool. We also recognize that these medicines hold deep spiritual and cultural significance for many Indigenous communities that Western medicine and society may never truly understand. As such, tools are only helpful with proper training and support. It can be fun to go on a trip, but the experiences we have along the way can be intense, confusing, and unsettling. That's where qualified therapists or guides come in. Psychedelics can bring us experiences of profound connectedness, but they aren't categorically helpful, for example, when it comes to reintegrating trauma energy that's been stored in the body. Medicines can help us feel better, which is fine, but a holistic approach to spirituality also involves rewriting our internal programs and doing the long-wave work of integrating individual, communal, ancestral, and spiritual information.

People who suffer from trauma often seek relief through spirituality. Spiritual practices can ease our suffering, but the relief is only short-term if we're attempting to escape or cling to the spiritual dimension in a disembodied way. Trying to bypass our worldly experiences is a clear sign of nonintegrated spiritual practice. We can't deal with the world—it's too hopeless, noisy, mean, unspiritual—so we do everything we can to shut it out or get away.

We can be quite troubled in life and still access higher realms and blissful experiences through psychedelics or meditation, but we eventually have to come back to a more mundane existence. That can be problematic if we can't reconcile the two realms or if we value the spiritual and denigrate the worldly. A lot of people who've been traumatized want to care less about this place. They want to care less about people, and they want to care less about this planet and life. But when we begin healing our trauma and our Self begins to become more prominent, we can align our Self-energy with our spiritual experiences and use all of it to become more present, caring, and mindful in the world. It's a matter of embodiment and connection.

Remember that Self-energy is contagious. The more Self-energy we can bring into our relationships and interactions with the world, the better. When we begin to understand that everything is interdependent, we naturally gravitate toward an integrated approach to healing. We no longer feel as interested in bypassing any of our experiences, and we understand that our health and the health of the world are intertwined. We are not isolated beings living atop a dead planet; we *are* the planet. Conceiving of ourselves as separate from the greater biosphere has led to tremendous harm to ourselves, others, and the planet all of us comprise and share. Ideally, our spiritual practices work to heal this unnatural split.

Falling in Love with the Path

One common pitfall among spiritual seekers is looking too far ahead. It's tempting to place most of our emphasis on arriving at that special place down the road, be it called Heaven, Nirvana, Jannah, enlightenment, divine union, or something else. But focusing too much on the result can be another form of escape, another defense mechanism against our pain.

That's okay because we need to find a way to deal with our pain, but in the end, presence is a more fruitful path than only looking forward to the end state—being *with* our pain, being *with* our defense mechanisms, *with* our protectors and exiles, *with* our trauma, *with* our burdens. Ideally, we sign up for the journey, for walking instead of arriving, for experiencing instead of reaping the future benefits of our experiences. For some, traveling through life this way is the ultimate commitment to the Divine. The world isn't some afflicted realm or obstacle. It is worthy of our love, presence, and devotion.

All the difficult stuff we experience along the path—our messy emotions, for example—aren't in the way. We don't feel those emotions in order to make them disappear. We feel them because we're alive and because being alive entails emotions. When I'm scared, I'm scared. When I'm full of fear, I feel fear. It's the same when I'm happy, sad, angry, or lost. All our humanness is part of the path, and there's tremendous power and beauty to loving the path.

Conclusion

We all live with some accumulation of individual, collective, and ancestral trauma. We clearly see how this cycle of repetition continues to impact our societies, manifesting as ongoing conflicts, wars, racism, and political systems that hoard power for the few at the expense of the many. Too many societies are based on frozen information stuck in the past, and everything that's frozen in the past is repetitive. The unintegrated history repeats itself in our political conversations, social issues, global conflicts, and climate crisis. As these patterns continue, so too do the impacts of trauma over time. One response to this is to shrug, look the other way, and say, "That's just how the world is. That's just how people are."

But that's not how people are. That's only how we are when we live generation after generation in a world that's unable to heal from its trauma. The damaging experiences former generations couldn't integrate have been split off and disembodied, becoming the ghosts of our societies. All that experiential data didn't disappear in the past. It's stored somewhere within us. There's an architecture in the collective unconscious in which the transgressor and transgressed remain entangled, and it will remain that way until the energy can update itself and heal.

To live together in an emergent, creative future of possibility, we need to address our legacy burdens. We must find a way to stop doing the same things over and over again. Societal processes tend to repeat themselves. Maybe we can't get rid of them entirely, but we *can* re-own and reintegrate the ghosts of the past.

Relating is a data flow. As data flows, we feel connected and can resonate with each other. Even when we disagree on things, we can hold space for disagreement and explore them. We're capable of making space for contradictions. Unfortunately, trauma creates places in us where we are numb or absent, and that results in inverted data. There's plenty of information; it's just not available to the collective. Invariably, social struggles of all kinds happen because of this. Numbness and absence are important functions that we need to learn to work with in order to bring essential information back to life.

When we commit to individual healing, that effort ripples out like a wave into the collective. Any healing work releases the past. We integrate the root causes of trauma, which helps us open up and become present, fresh, creative, loving, innovative, and connective. Everybody who does their inner work or releases legacy burdens or intergenerational trauma contributes to changes in the larger world.

There is exponential power in collective attunement. A group's unified presence can create a field that supports deeper healing, but only when its constituents have a relatively stable inner state. Ultimately, we can work toward holding an awareness of our own state while also being attuned to the dynamics unfolding within the group. Of course, it's often necessary to attend to our individual trauma first. Once we're more grounded in our personal lives, we can have more resources to tend to collective and ancestral traumas—our own as well as others'.

Spaces for Collective Healing

Sometimes when we're traumatized, we're convinced we need to heal alone, especially if we've grown up in cultures that encourage a hyper-individualized mindset. It's true that we all have our burdens to bear (and to heal) in life, but that doesn't mean we have to do it alone. Our nervous systems are relational. Because we evolved as communal beings, relational holding spaces are paramount. Groups that come together with an intention to grow and heal as one mean more collective intelligence, and attuning to healthy ecosystems with increased intelligence can bring about new patterns and exponential change.

To move toward the level of healing required to meet the challenges of our current metacrisis, collective healing spaces are needed. To create widespread change, we need structural change. That means we need to translate this work into policy, into realms that are capable of funding and sustaining the development of healing architecture in our societies. In particular, we need to implement spaces that are intentionally designed to help us process our legacy burdens and collective trauma. This isn't optional; it's essential. Among other benefits, spaces like these could significantly reduce healthcare costs, crime rates, addiction, social fragmentation, and polarization. They would also support the healing of core wounds that perpetuate institutional racism across generations. Every government, ideally, would take responsibility for its burdens and trauma layers by supporting these foundational healing practices and developing such spaces for its citizens.

We know too much about trauma to not act and develop these systems of healing. If we are to serve future generations, healing must become a collective skill. Together, with governments and existing institutions, we can build systems of collective healing and catalyze the post-traumatic learning and maturation that our societies so deeply need.

We're not there yet. Unfortunately, many of our governments seem more inclined to ignore social ills than address them in any substantive manner. As our societies work to develop more favorable architecture, we can be the ones who initiate as many social healing spaces as we can. As we work on convincing our leaders that this is in our best interests, we must begin the work ourselves, which means developing the frameworks, gathering convincing research, and cultivating favorable methodologies and rituals. Dance, movement practices, music, and art are part of this too. Whatever we do, it's crucial that we continue to promote larger social structures dedicated to healing.

Practice

REFLECTIONS AND INTENTIONS

As we conclude this book, take a few deep breaths. Every time you breathe out, see if you can make the exhalation a little slower or longer. That will help your nervous system slowly down-regulate and switch into a reflective state.

Notice where your body feels most lively, energized, streaming, pulsing, or tingling. Honor all the information that is stored in your body, all the achievements of humanity that reside within you. All the learning from all the trauma and healing from previous generations sits in every cell of your body. That wisdom is in your body, your psyche, and in the communities and social structures we build together. Feel the truth of that.

For a moment, reflect on your life and the communities to which you belong. What practices or reflections did you encounter in this book that you can carry forward? Which ones would you like to revisit or share with others?

After you've considered that for a minute or so, return your awareness to your physical sensations. As you pay attention there, also notice that which is aware of those sensations. You can feel what's happening in your body, and you can notice the awareness that does so. Whatever we call it, this awareness has a timeless dimension to it, a depth that's hard to measure. Gently take a couple of deeper breaths and really sense into this awareness.

After a minute or so more, open your eyes. Sometimes when we conclude a practice and open our eyes, we disconnect from our internal experiences and place all our attention outside. For this practice, try to remain connected to your inner world—your sensations, reflections, permeating awareness, and so on—with your eyes open. Set an intention to bring this presence, this wisdom, to anyone or anything that needs your attention and assistance. Remember that nothing you do or feel or think happens in isolation. You are interdependent with others, with the collective field. Together, in our collective presence, there is nothing we cannot heal.

Appendix for Therapists

The archetypal path of the healer is also spiritual. If we view it as such, we can learn and grow from every interaction, be it therapeutic or otherwise, and that will clarify and expand our own lives, our own universe. Over time, old challenges will feel less obstructive, and we'll meet new ones with increased openness, wisdom, and presence. One definition of wisdom is how much of the world we can host in ourselves. The more space we can host, the more fluid our relationships become and the less othering we do. That said, our work as therapists wouldn't be nearly as rewarding without regular challenges from our clients and ourselves.

Practice

CLIENTS (OR OTHER PEOPLE) WHO TRIGGER YOUR PROTECTORS—DICK

I invite you to think of a person—and for therapists, it could be a client—who triggers your protectors in a way you're not happy with. If you can't think of anybody, then God bless you, you're already enlightened, but if you have somebody in mind, then visualize putting that person in a comfortable, contained room. Imagine the room has a window in it so you can see the person, but maybe they can't see you.

While this person is in that contained room, have them do or say the thing that triggers your protector. Just notice what happens in your body and mind as you get triggered. Notice the thoughts, beliefs, sensations, and emotions that come rushing in when this person says or does this thing and notice how much your reactions overwhelm you and take over. Now, let me reassure you that you're not going to go into that room in this exercise, so it's safe to focus on the protector that came up so strongly. Let it know you're not going to be dealing with this person, so it can stand down and separate from you a little. Then, find where this protector seems to be located in your body and see if you can get curious about why it jumps up so much with this particular person.

Inquire from a place of pure curiosity and wait for the answer to come. Don't think of the answer, just see what comes. What's it afraid would happen if it didn't jump up to protect you this way? If it answers that question, then you probably learned something about the part itself, the parts it protects, or other parts that it's afraid might come in otherwise. And if that's true, then go ahead and extend appreciation to it for trying to protect you in this way. Even if it gets in your way, just let it know that you get that it's committed to keeping you safe. See how it reacts to your appreciation.

Another question you can ask this part is: how old does it think you are? Not how old it is, but how old does it think you are. And again, wait for the answer. If it got your age wrong, then go ahead and update it and see how it reacts to that. Maybe you can handle more than it thought you could. Then, you could ask another question: If you could heal or change what it's protecting so this protective role wouldn't be as necessary and it could do something else, what might it like to do instead?

The final question you can ask is: What does it need from you going forward? Again, don't think, just wait for the answers to come. When that feels complete, thank the part for whatever it shared with you and begin to shift your focus back to the present moment, taking deep breaths if that feels right.

Live Session: Dick and Thomas with Participant

Participant: I'm a somatic therapist. I've recently got into IFS training, and I notice that clients sometimes cycle through the history of their trauma, and it can be hard to bring them into an embodied relational presence. I'm curious about the parts that show up in me that feel like they really want to help when it can feel so frustrating. How can I support those clients while also not getting in the way of a natural process?

Dick: You're not alone among therapists who have these parts that desperately want to help, and they can sometimes get in the way. And there are clients who will fill up the session with stories about their traumas, and it seems like they're doing work, but it can also keep you away from the exiles that need their attention. They're stuck in the traumas. There aren't that many times where I'm forcefully directive as a therapist, but if I do feel like that's what's happening, I'll say something like, "We really need this part that's telling the story to relax back and just let us go to these places in your body or around your body." I'll be a little bit assertive that way.

If you can do it with Self-energy, people will hear the compassion in your voice so they won't get as reactive.

Thomas: I would say something similar, but maybe a little bit different. First of all, I would look in myself. What is actually happening in me that gets a bit annoyed? Why might I have that reaction when the person is talking, talking, talking and not really going into embodiment? I stay present with whatever comes up. If something triggers you, that's interesting, and I recommend you look into it. Second, I think it's worth considering that something in the client needs to talk a lot to keep the relationship a bit distant to stay safe. If that's the case, then maybe at a certain time, I would explore that with the client. What function does the talking fulfill? Exploring that together can deepen the relationship. You want to help them, which is lovely. I mean, we all do this job, I think, because we are in service to people. But I don't think that's what's getting in the way. That something else coming up in you needs to be seen, and you can do that with Self-energy, as Dick says, and offer that back to your clients. What do you think is coming up in you when that happens?

Participant: What came up in the exercise Dick just led is that there are two parts. One is a kind of anxious part that feels, "Oh, other people's suffering is painful." It's almost too much. I want to shift away from the suffering. And because that part isn't comfortable, it's like, "Oh, how can I decrease their suffering?" Then there's a part that gets irritated. Maybe it's a protector for that anxious part. It thinks, "This is too much." or "We're not getting anywhere. We need to get somewhere."

Thomas: Right. And maybe if you give that anxious part a little space and say, "Okay, I'm getting anxious here. I'm becoming a bit shaky and anxious that you are not getting anywhere." Let that breathe for a moment if that's accessible now.

Participant: Yeah, I can sense the feelings underneath. It's like the feeling level. Suffering by nature is painful.

Thomas: That's the thought process. When you say, "Suffering is painful," that's a thought. And then you can see what's actually the feeling, what's really the feeling that comes with that thought? Always take into account that sometimes the feeling is an absence of feeling or maybe a numbness.

Participant: I can sense a thread into the feeling, and I can sense the numbness.

Thomas: Exactly.

Participant: And it's more of a foreground feeling.

Thomas: Then you can say, "Oh, maybe in these moments I go a bit numb," and then, "I respect the numbness." Then, let that numbness be because that's a sign that you touched an overwhelmed part, and maybe just breathe. The numbness has a space and is being honored.

Participant: Yeah, and I can feel some relief like, "Oh, that's allowed."

Thomas: Exactly. And then you can see what changes when that numbness is allowed, and it can slowly lead to a relief or also a bit of grounding. It opens a bit of space inside and maybe another layer then comes.

Participant: Yeah, I'm surprised that the layer is there. I'm aware that being in a live space, I'm aware the protective layer feels maybe stronger. So I'm sensing it more like a thread, but it's like a thread into my kind of organ/body that feels like a young part that's like, "Oh, please be with me." Like it wants contact.

Thomas: Just maybe one more step, and then we can also let it rest in here. Either with your eyes open or closed, touch the place that says, "Be with me." Maybe there's a sense that I feel you, that I also feel you in this shaky part, and you can feel that we are feeling this together.

Participant: Yeah. There's a kind of . . . I can feel that part's like, "Oh, that's possible." That's the feeling, like a waking up.

Thomas: Right. Let's feel that, that something is opening up and you feel, "Oh, that's possible." And even a little bit of joy to be felt in this place, recognizing that there's a togetherness.

Participant: I feel a grounding through my body, and I feel myself. Like I can lean in.

Thomas: That you allow yourself to lean in, to feel that. Something gets nourished. You're leaning in. Something is being felt, seen, nourished, and can ground itself then in your body.

Participant: It's much more connected through my body.

Thomas: That's beautiful. You're showing us something I think maybe a group of us who work with clients might see as a trigger, when our clients are somehow not reachable. When a client is available, our relational flow is there. But when a client's not available, then it might trigger the parts of us that didn't get nourished at the beginning of our life, and then we start to get a bit agitated. I think what you showed us now is that you can lean in and let that part get what it needs. You can ground yourself and provide that space to people who aren't reachable because it triggers you less and less, and then you will be in what Dick calls Self-energy.

Participant: Yeah, I'm feeling that available now. Thank you.

Thomas: Thank you.

Dick: That was beautiful. I continue to remark about how similarly we're working. In IFS terms, you honored this protector and then asked about what it protects, which brought you to the exile it protects. Then you went to that exile and formed a caring relationship with it. It's amazing.

Thomas: Beautiful. Thank you for noticing that.

Participant: Thanks to the both of you.

DICK'S REFLECTIONS FOR THERAPISTS

As a therapist, once you learn that someone you're working with has a part that doesn't trust you, it will often call up a protector in your system who wants to change that part's mind and convince it to trust you. Generally, that's a mistake. Instead, I recommend letting that part know that you recognize it probably has plenty of good reasons not to trust anyone, including you. It's also the boss. It gets to decide what's untrustworthy. Over time, keep checking in with it. It can help to ask what it would look like for it to trust you, but it's more important to honor its role as a protector and recognize how it took care of the person who got betrayed or hurt in such a deep way that trust was no longer an option. But I strongly advise against putting any pressure on it to trust you.

As a therapist, it's not uncommon to feel bad or "off" during or after a session. Sometimes it's because one of your parts gets triggered by a client, sometimes it's because your critic is on your back, or maybe there's an advisor part that wants to call your attention to a misstep you've made and genuinely wants to help you do better. When this happens, check in with yourself and find out what's going on. If there is an exile or protector involved, maybe you can work with it in the moment. Or maybe you'll decide to wait until later and get help from a colleague.

In the process of doing that, it's important to not blame your client. When we get triggered by somebody, it's crucial—especially if it involves a part that needs unburdening—to follow that trailhead and see where there's any stuckness in the past. Once you discover that, you can begin to heal those parts. Over time, you'll become less triggered and more able to hold Self-energy, even in the face of all kinds of emotions. Maybe your client resembled one of your parts and another part of you that hates that part is going to make it hard for you to stay in Self. And if you have an attitude toward a lot of your parts, that's going to play out when your client (or child, spouse, parent, etc.) resembles those parts. The more you can heal your parts, the less trauma will get played out in the external world.

I think of people who trigger me as "tor-mentors." That hyphen between *tor* and *mentor* is to remind me that those people are mentoring me about what I need to heal. If a client brings up something strong in me, I know there's a part that needs attention. It's not the Self because the Self doesn't take stuff in. But most of us have parts that learned to play safe by bringing in certain emotions from our parents and other caregivers and calling them our own. This is how we end up with other people's burdens. For this reason, tor-mentors are good news! Without them, it would be a lot harder to know where we most need healing.

THOMAS'S REFLECTIONS FOR THERAPISTS

In our work, it's best not to pathologize sessions and interactions we walk away from feeling like, "That didn't go so well" or "We're not getting anywhere" or "I'm not sure what I'm doing," or whatever your flavor of that experience was. Instead of getting too heavy about it, try to view it as a learning edge, an invitation to self-reflection. Every difficult client or group interaction is a signpost of growth and the expansion of our own conscious universe. These moments, even when uncomfortable, are accelerators for our own development if we integrate the underlying parts.

When these situations occur, taking out your journal or meditating can be useful to digest the experience. Through gentle contemplation, with compassion for yourself, you can usually discover what dynamics were at play, but sometimes peer support or supervision may help you understand more. Talking with another therapist often clarifies the situation and may lead to a better solution than you would come up with on your own. Supervision invites leadership, and you can lean on someone you trust who has more experience than you to bring the heart of the matter to the fore. And that's part of the beauty of this work. Ideally, we're all committed to lifelong development, and we help each other become clearer, kinder, and wiser as we take this journey alongside one another.

A supportive relationship is as requisite for therapists as it is for clients. The relationship between nervous systems means everything. Especially when younger parts of us are involved, safe and modulated environments are crucial. Just as we can provide the type of environments that were missing in our clients' lives, we need to provide the same for each other.

In the previous live session, I tuned into the client's numbness and demonstrated my willingness to be there with it. Together, we created a space in which the numbness was welcome. I believe all our emotions are shared landscapes; there's no such thing as a purely personal emotion. We feel emotions individually, of course, but we're also designed to experience them in a shared field, like when a child is overcome with fear and co-regulates with their parents. Ideally, the nervous systems of the parents and child share that experience of fear and process it together. When a parent sees the child's fear, acknowledges it, and embraces the child, the emotional bodies involved become synchronized. The parent says, "I feel that you're afraid. Come here, my love. Together, let's look at what's happening." This is quite different from telling the child to stop being afraid by saying something like, "There's nothing to be concerned about. Go to sleep." We're meant to experience fear, anger, shame, numbness, and whatever else in a mutual landscape. We feel what comes up together, and then we feel safe enough to move forward or experience other, maybe deeper, feelings.

This level of co-regulation is our goal in serving our clients. It can be challenging at times, which is why grounding is so important, especially for those of us with sensitive nervous systems. I think of it like a tree. If a tree has a crown of branches and leaves that are far larger than its root system, that tree will always be shaky. But a tree with roots that extend deep and wide can withstand all sorts of winds and storms without becoming structurally disturbed. If you devote yourself to grounding and clearing your interior space before, during, and after sessions, your presence will become stronger, more palpable, and better able to stand both firm and pliable for your clients and others. You can be present with anything that occurs in the therapeutic space, and fundamentally, it will trouble you less. The energy will move through you, and you won't hold it nearly as much.

Appendix for Group Facilitators

We believe the next stage of trauma work needs to prioritize collective unburdening and collective healing. Yes, individual-based therapy is essential, but considering that we're all interdependently affected by our ancestries, communities, and cultures, it's imperative that we expand the current map of trauma healing. Large-scale, accessible, and lasting change must come through collective resilience and connection. That means skillful group work by present, Self-led facilitators.

Those of us who want to play more prominent roles in collective healing need to be doubly mindful of unburdening ourselves. Self-awareness and self-regulation are essential when leading group work. By emphasizing our own clarity and transparency, we can prevent ourselves from projecting our unresolved issues onto groups, helping to maintain the integrity of the collective process. Our own inward focus allows participants to process their emotions, find grounding, and bring more clarity and presence back into the group space. In this way, our self-work can contribute to a more coherent and open field within the group.

DICK ON GROUP WORK

From the IFS perspective, it's crucial for a group facilitator to develop an awareness of when you're in Self and when you're not. At the same time you're monitoring group dynamics, you're also noticing what's coming up in you and how much Self-energy you're feeling and expressing. This can be as straightforward as monitoring those eight C qualities I listed in chapter 1: curiosity, confidence, calmness, compassion, creativity, courage, clarity, and connectedness. How well are you able to feel those qualities as you work with the group? Sometimes the answer will be "not very well."

Even experienced facilitators have challenging days. When that happens, it's okay to ask for a timeout while you investigate what's going on for you and engage in the requisite parts work. Sometimes that's as simple as asking a triggered part to recede for a little while so you can continue to work effectively with the group. If you let that part know you're going to come back later to follow up with them, they're much more likely to give you the space you need in the moment. The more you work with parts and develop your relationship with them, the more they'll trust the Self and become team-oriented when you ask them to be.

The more Self-energy you bring to facilitation, the more it will positively affect the groups you work with, helping other group members feel safe enough to be vulnerable and access their exiles. The more this occurs in a group, the more contagious the Self-energy becomes. Ideally, your facilitation fosters a large field in which all parts feel welcome and judgment and triggers occur at a workable minimum. That's a good description of what healing collective work looks and feels like.

THOMAS ON GROUP WORK

Groups—and the dynamics that emerge in collective presence—are microcosms of society. As such, they reveal our larger human challenges and possibilities. Groups are living systems, coherent fields that can foster deep healing and growth when there is alignment and attunement among the participants. There is a shared intelligence when everyone in a room is aware of the group and the group becomes aware of its own process. By healing and evolving together in groups like these, we catalyze broader societal transformation. The ripple effects are palpable and evident; the collective field acts as a contagion for positive and impactful change.

Facilitating a group requires that I remain aware of my internal process as well as what's going on in the group field—the experiences of the participants and the composite "whole" that is created together. We call this a "we" space. An effective facilitator needs to develop the competencies to sense fluctuations in the field, adapt accordingly, and determine what words and actions will best foster healing and presence. This is especially critical in large-scale processes in which we're addressing and unpacking collective social wounds. To this end, I developed the Collective Trauma Integration Process (CTIP), which I explain more in depth in my book *Healing Collective Trauma*. CTIP is a methodology that focuses on integrating the trauma that stems from social tragedies that impact multiple generations, such as war, genocide, systemic oppression, natural disasters, and cultural disruptions. The core principles and components of CTIP include:

- **Understanding Collective Trauma** (examined extensively in chapter 3).

- **The Integration Process:** After opening a space to address collective trauma and its impacts, the next step is to create a safe and attuned space for participants to witness and resonate with each other's experiences. The goal is to invite the group to remain present with difficult emotions and sensations and facilitate the repair of any ruptures by rebuilding trust and integrating the fragmented aspects of the collective psyche.

- **Key Tools and Practices:** These include meditation, somatic awareness practices, group resonance (in which the shared presence of the group creates a powerful space for healing), facilitated group sharing, transparent communication, and methods to integrate the transgenerational transmission of trauma.

- **Core Goals:** The core work of the CTIP is to heal the past by integrating unresolved trauma, building individual and communal resilience, fostering unity by reconnecting people to a shared sense of humanity, inducing post-traumatic growth and learning, and supporting systemic change by creating new paradigms of healing and cooperation.

Through my nongovernmental organization (NGO), The Pocket Project, which I cofounded with my wife, Yehudit Sasportas, we organized a series of labs, or group meetings, with hundreds of participants who took part in CTIP sessions. Launched in 2020, these labs address specific cultures group identities, causes, and social justice movements. We have large therapist teams in these groups that can offer one-on-one work. Some of the more notable applications have involved group healing after natural disasters and working on colonial and racial wounds in Germany with the descendants of the survivors and perpetrators of the Holocaust (mentioned in chapter 6).

When I begin working with a group—be it a handful of executives or hundreds of people whose families were directly involved or harmed by the Holocaust—I start by encouraging relational synchronization among the group's members through exercises and centering practices. When it feels like the group has arrived at enough coherence, we set an intention to look at whatever collective trauma field fits with that cultural space. Then, we pay attention to whatever collective unconscious material shows up in the field. The more we witness that and listen to each other, the more we're able to re-embody disembodied ghosts and exiled or absent information and begin to integrate them.

Collective spaces inherently engage in collective witnessing, but on a larger scale, fragmentation prevents the society or population from being aware of this witnessing capacity. In the groups I've led, a strong witnessing space often emerges, and that's what it takes for collective healing to unfold. The facilitator's intention, together with coherence and group resonance, will often jump-start a larger process. The moment we set an intention in a synchronized group, almost immediately any absence or woundedness of that culture appears in the room. There is often a wide variety of sensations and experiences that are felt throughout the group space. Sleepiness and the inability to stay present are just a couple examples of this.

Whatever comes up in the group, we honor the intelligence of this process. Sometimes people experience waves of emotion that ripple through the group. Sometimes images or vivid memories surface. All of these responses are emotions associated with the particular collective trauma that is expressing itself in the room.

In addition to the outpouring of emotions, people may shut down or experience numbness. By viewing defense mechanisms and protector energies with compassion, we're already displaying the awareness that fosters their integration. We see them for what they are, acknowledge their purpose, integrate them, and travel deeper into our own embodiment. It's no use hoping for protectors and defense mechanisms to never appear or make themselves known; we actually need them to fully mature and heal from our trauma.

Through this process, we can go deeper and deeper, such that the group itself becomes like a magic pond in which more and more from the collective cultural trauma can bubble up. Once we as a group recognize that certain symptoms in the room reflect a collective defense mechanism, people start to feel things. At this time, people might talk about their individual experiences, but they might actually express something ancestral or collective. When we're in trauma zones, it's terribly difficult to hear each other. For this reason, we encourage a lot of deep listening. Our collective health depends on how deeply we hear each other. Of course, some degree of success depends on how resourced and experienced a group is, as well as the structural safety experienced by the group.

When groups dive into far-reaching transgressions—be it the Holocaust, gender violence, colonialism, or patriarchy—it's also beneficial to have people involved who aren't directly affected. People who don't share the same cultural background are also helpful in holding a witnessing space so there's more capacity in the room. We open something, integrate it a little bit, and then reflect. We offer presence to the various voices, increase the collective awareness, and gradually strengthen the resources of the group.

About the Authors

Dr Richard C. Schwartz earned his PhD in marriage and family therapy at Purdue University, subsequently working as an associate professor at the Institute for Juvenile Research at the University of Illinois and later at the Family Institute at Northwestern University. Over time, Dick developed Internal Family Systems (IFS) Therapy after years of working with clients and operating on the assumption that personality isn't a monolith, but something comprised of multiple parts. He observed that these parts usually caused his clients problems when they were ignored, but that they were more helpful and compliant when they were attended to, respected, and had their needs addressed. Specifically, IFS was developed to put clients in charge of their therapy and recovery. IFS empowers clients to build self-acceptance, internal harmony, and self-leadership. The modality is particularly known for its effectiveness with people experiencing trauma, and IFS can be applied in individual, couple, or group settings. Dick founded the Center for Self Leadership in 2000 to offer IFS trainings to professionals. It later became IFS Institute and continues to expand access to the model worldwide. For more information about Dick and the Institute's growing number of courses and resources, or to find an IFS Practitioner to work with, visit IFS-Institute.com.

Dr Thomas Hübl is a renowned teacher, author, and international facilitator who works within the complexity of systems and cultural change, integrating the core insights of great wisdom traditions and mysticism with the discoveries of science. Since the early 2000s, he has led large-scale events and courses on the healing of collective trauma. He is the author of *Attuned: Practicing Interdependence to Heal Our Trauma—and Our World* and *Healing Collective Trauma: A Process for Integrating Our Intergenerational and Cultural Wounds*. Hübl has served as an advisor and guest faculty for universities and organizations, as a coach for CEOs and organizational leaders, and is currently a visiting scholar at the Wyss Institute at Harvard University. He is the cofounder of the Pocket Project, an NGO dedicated to grassroots collective trauma work worldwide, and the Global Restoration Institute, which provides diplomatic training and advising to support the development of trauma-informed organizations and governments. Learn more at thomashuebl.com.